How to Make Love While Conscious

How to
Make Love
While Conscious

SEX AND SOBRIETY

Guy Kettelhack

A HAZELDEN BOOK

HarperSanFrancisco
A Division of HarperCollins*Publishers*

The first-person stories in this book accurately reflect the feelings, experiences, and circumstances expressed by recovering individuals, but all names, locations, and identifying details have been changed.

FIRST EDITION

Library of Congress Cataloging-in-Publication Data
Kettelhack, Guy.
How to make love while conscious : sex & sobriety /
Guy Kettelhack. — 1st ed.
    p. cm.
"A Hazelden Book."
    1. Recovering alcoholics—Sexual behavior. 2. Recovering addicts—Sexual behavior. 3. Sex (Psychology). I. Title.
HV5201.S48K48 1993
362.29'13—dc20   92-56424
                                                                      CIP

ISBN 0-06-250662-5 (acid-free paper)

  93 94 95 96 97 ❖ RRD(H) 10 9 8 7 6 5 4 3 2 1

This edition is printed on acid-free paper that meets the American National Standards Institute Z39.48 Standard.

For Bob,
my brother

My role here is what it has been in every book about recovery I've been privileged to work on: I'm a recovering alcoholic, enthralled by the miracle of sobriety, attempting to report on it—not an "expert." I'm struggling as much as anyone else with the issues I write about: we're all in this together. The book's content and tone derive from a sense of shared struggle and quest. While this is not a book that offers any kind of explicit guide to the Twelve Steps, it *is* written in the spirit of Twelve-Step recovery. The women and men you'll meet here have all benefited from the healing that Twelve-Step recovery makes possible for thousands of alcoholics and addicts. However, if you're still on the fence about Twelve-Step recovery, I don't think you'll feel excluded. The experiences, circumstances, and feelings of the people here cover a wide range. However we may label ourselves, whatever process of recovery we may be pursuing, there's room for everyone on this voyage—including you. In the great diversity of voices you'll find here, I hope and expect that you'll be able to find an echo of your own voice.

GUY KETTELHACK
New York, 1993

CONTENTS

CHAPTER 1

The Burning Point

Love is the burning point of life.
JOSEPH CAMPBELL

The burning point of life. Warmth that nurtures, fire that destroys. Uncontrollable, by unpredictable turns brilliant, blinding, illuminating, terrifying, welcoming. A beam that incises the heart, with the power to sever and to mend.

What Joseph Campbell says about love can as easily be said of sex. The word burns: despite its ubiquity, *sex* may still be the most charged word in the English language. Certainly for recovering addicts and alcoholics the word seems to be laden with even more than the usual considerable baggage it carries for just about everyone else living in Western civilization.

Sobriety is an astonishing, revelatory, wonderful gift; few recovering alcoholics and drug addicts who've managed to stay sober for any length of time would disagree with this. But despite our newfound clarity, few of us escape having problems with sex, intimacy, and love. We can no longer ignore our painful blocks, and our fears can sometimes loom larger when we're not escaping them through booze and/or drugs: fears, for example, that in that last binge (or at any time during the past two, five, ten years when you were out of control), you might have contracted AIDS. Fears of taking the HIV test. Fears of even contemplating the prospect of an intimate relationship with anyone, sober. Fears that you'll never be able to open up physically and emotionally to another person the way you wish you could. Fears that though other people seem to have learned how to integrate sex with love, you can't. Even in the context of your recovery, of your sobriety that you wouldn't give up for anything, you may not be able to imagine *ever* opening up completely and connecting fully and satisfyingly with another human being. It's not that you don't want to; you do, desperately. But something keeps blocking you. Worse, that something seems to mean something's wrong with *you*. You can't help thinking, "This is all my fault."

And who is there, really, to talk to about all this? One young recovering alcoholic, Daniel, remembers trying to bring up in an Alcoholics Anonymous meeting the problems he'd had with impotency ever since he'd given up drinking a year before. "You could have cut the tension with a knife," he says. "It's like everyone turned to ice. Later, some guy came up to me and told me in no uncertain terms that sex wasn't an appropriate topic for an AA meeting. I felt crushed and ashamed." Daniel has since heard that it *is* appropriate to bring up his sexual fears in the context of AA, at least to a sponsor, close AA friend, or therapist, and even to broach the topic at some AA meetings. In fact, not doing so could threaten his sobriety. As he says, "I always used booze as an aphrodisiac. Sex and alcohol were completely linked. I *have* to talk about it to someone."

The secrets so many of us harbor about our sexual and romantic lives can eat away at our self-esteem and serenity and, sooner or later, put our very sobriety into jeopardy. It's clear from my conversations with scores of recovering men and women, old and young, straight and gay, rich and poor, black and white, of every ethnicity and social and economic background, that finding ways to investigate and talk about these secrets is an urgent necessity. For most people, sobriety seems almost to require facing our most intimate, vulnerable, and private selves. It's what's meant by the Twelve-Step slogan, "We're only as sick as our secrets." It isn't that the content of our secrets is "sick," but rather that the secretness itself is the problem. We wouldn't hide if we weren't terrified of being known, or if we hadn't judged our secrets as being too terrible to share. There may be no more crippling obstacles to our serenity than the fear and judgment we bring to the whole sexual arena.

Sobriety is progressively illuminating: it seems to want to shed light on everything, especially those parts of us we've striven most to hide. However, the resistance we put up to this progressive illumination can be formidable. As much a miracle as our sober consciousness is, it is neither rose-tinted nor selective. Its burning point is as powerful and relentless as Joseph Campbell's fire of love, bringing with it an all-encompassing clarity that initially can be terrifying, especially when we focus on our sexual fears, memories, fantasies, secrets, hopes, and expectations.

Sex is the topic, the guiding focus for this book because it is the magnet for so much of our anxiety. I have yet to meet a recovering addict or alcoholic who doesn't ache for reassurance and help in this fearful, shame-ridden realm, loath as most of us are to ask for it. Most of us suffer to some degree from shaky or low self-esteem, from a deeply ingrained self-mistrust that convinces us we are unlovable, unattractive, less than, inadequate. All of these sparks of self-doubt roar into a blaze in the area of sex. Our lack of self-esteem is manifest in our need to compensate for it, by seeking sexual partners compulsively, like trophies that prove an attractiveness we can't seem to believe about ourselves; or in how we sequester ourselves in a locked-up celibacy, a withdrawn and fearful state that ensures no one can ever get in. The fearful ways in which we face the prospect of sex vary as symptoms of what is undeniably a deeper set of problems. But sex remains an extremely effective diving board into the self because, maybe more than any other aspect of our lives, it is so primally, directly, and revealingly connected to how we *feel* about ourselves.

Exploring this territory seems to require becoming conscious in a special way. In fact, what I mean by the word *conscious*, as well as the terms *how to* and *make love*, departs considerably from conventional definitions.

A NEW TAKE ON *HOW TO*, *MAKE LOVE*, AND *CONSCIOUS*

How to Make Love While Conscious is a book that defines its terms in some singular ways.

The *how to* in this book grows out of who you are. You won't find bulleted sex therapy exercises or worksheets on "Ten Ways to Get Sexy, Thin, and Rich" here. This is a self-help book that quite literally lives up to the term *self*-help. By encouraging an inner process of self-knowledge, through the example of scores of other recovering people who've undergone this process themselves, a goal in these pages is to help you to become more self-aware and self-accepting, which includes more sexually self-aware and self-accepting. In other words, the *how to* will evolve from an exploration and acceptance of who you are, not who you think you're supposed to be or would be if only you were a better person or lived the way your mother wanted you to live, but who you really are.

The *make love* part doesn't only mean having sex. Certainly our focus and point of departure in this book is sex, but sex as a magnet for some very charged and often terribly negative feelings many recovering addicts and alcoholics have learned to have about themselves, feelings that can profoundly block our progress in sobriety and interfere with our ability to live satisfying, fulfilling lives. Our route in this book starts out with sex as a sort of passport, a means of entry; our destinations end up being far wider. How you feel about your body, issues about intimacy, love, self-esteem, shame, secrecy—all of these mark our voyage in this book and go far beyond the entryway marked "sex."

Making love—creating (feeling, finding, nurturing, enjoying) love—seems to be the product of some careful tending of the soul's soil. Recovering people teach me that I need to love myself before I can love anybody else, and that the process of reaching out in any kind of intimate way to anybody else means first of all having a clear sense of who is doing the reaching and what is being sought. All of which brings us to the word *conscious*, which is to me interchangeable with *sober*. A central premise of this book is that simply by putting down drugs and alcohol and taking some active measures to maintain sobriety (like attending Twelve-Step meetings), we put into process an organic growth and expansion. By ceasing to obliterate our thoughts and feelings with alcohol and drugs and other addictive behaviors, we open the door to an astonishingly wide and deep realm, one that encourages greater consciousness, in fact requires such consciousness for its own exploration. Simply put, sobriety breeds sobriety. Consciousness, from my experience and observations of many recovering addicts and alcoholics, increases exponentially if we just get out of our own way and *let* it. We experience some of our greatest blocks in the sexual arena because, for most of us, sex requires a degree of nakedness (psychic as well as physical) that few recovering people are willing to experience without the buffering, muting, fantasizing effects of drugs or alcohol.

Recovering alcoholics and addicts who've managed to face these blocks and allow themselves, slowly, to achieve a state of psychic and emotional nakedness have some surprising and reassuring messages to report about how the meaning of sex has changed in their lives. "Having sex for me now," one recovering alcoholic named Peter says, "is like going on a strange, long, unpredictable voyage. I end up feeling *everything*. Things come to me in waves. Sometimes I lose interest, or just feel gentle, or get in touch with fear or even anger. Other times it gets playful and I feel like a kid. Then I'll feel the most incredible even heart-breaking affection for my partner that I'll almost want to cry! At other times it's full of physical passion and lust. Sometimes in the course of making love to my wife, I'll lose my erection, worry about it, stop worrying about it, then allow new feelings to flood in and change me . . . It's just not about performance anymore. I suppose what's really going on is that a whole new language has come up between us, a new kind of communication." Peter is talking, obviously, about his experience of sex, but the attitude he's developed about his feelings during sex extends to other areas of his life as well. "You can't stop your feelings. It doesn't make sense to try, or to hate yourself for not being able, to control them. The

6

healing realization I've come to is that I don't have to fight myself anymore. I can be who I am; I can allow my feelings to flow through. A dividend is that I end up enjoying life more. Not in some zonked out state, like I was in when I drank. But with a sense of *richness*. A rounder sense of pleasure, one that allows everything from fear to rage to boredom to elation to pass through it. This emotional permissiveness hasn't only improved my sex life, it's improved my *life*, period."

Developing this emotional permissiveness is not easy. Our fear and trembling can stop us dead. There does not, however, seem to be any way out but through: to gain peace about our sexual selves, we seem to have to take a careful, detailed, attentive *look* at ourselves. Unfortunately, few books addressed to recovering addicts and alcoholics have trod this territory. My main frustration with much of the literature for alcoholics and addicts is that it doesn't reflect enough of the sheer confusion, terror, and messiness most of us feel about our lives, even in sobriety. A book about sex and sobriety isn't going to be very useful if it settles for pat conclusions or slogans or anything else offered as quick panaceas. What heals is the example of other people's honesty and courage in facing their secrets and fears: these can help us to find the courage to be honest about our own lives. This book grows out of pain, and as the Twelve-Step program I espouse has taught me, you can't begin to deal with pain if you can't bring yourself to look at it. True to this, you'll hear all manner of experience in this book. Some of it, in its particulars, may be pretty far from your own experience, but I hope much of it will echo the feelings and circumstances of your own sexual and emotional life. It won't all be pain; there's plenty of joy and revelation here, too. Nothing has been held back; holding back is what keeps our negative self-views so dangerously in place. In the spirit of the fourth Step of the Twelve Steps—"Made a searching and fearless moral inventory of ourselves"—this book invites you to make what may be the most fearless, searching, and rewarding inventory you have ever taken of yourself. And don't let the word *moral* scare you; you must define *moral* for yourself if it is to have any real meaning. No judgments will be passed here; rather, what this book offers is a great deal of experience, strength, and hope.

If the scores of women and men whose stories have fueled this book are any indication, you'll come out of this exploration with a new and much more satisfying sense of who you are. One of the dividends of this new self-knowledge ultimately seems to be that the how to's of your life, including your sexual life, begin slowly to sort themselves out, to suggest themselves to *you*. You may discover, as so many of the men and women in this book have discovered, that you can feel as good about developing your own sexual *how to* as you learn to feel more loving acceptance of yourself.

We live in a world so vastly more abundant than most of us have allowed ourselves to realize. My dearest hope is that this book will help you to tap into as much of that abundance as you can.

CHAPTER 2

Surrendering: Toward a New Sexual Honesty

Let's take a look now at three people who are encountering new ways to look at their sexual selves and experiences, and learning an important message about honesty. The idea of self-acceptance and getting honest about your feelings may sound familiar, right out of the last Twelve-Step meeting you went to. But getting honest about sex? You're not alone if you find that a forbidding prospect . . .

The first person you'll meet, Margaret, will introduce you to our primary concern at this stage: learning to get honest with yourself and revealing who you are to someone you trust. She will also give you an idea of how new insights can begin to alter some basic assumptions and behavior. Then Hiram and Dorothy will give us a more particular view of two demons Margaret shares with them: self-hatred and fear of connecting to other people.

But first, with Margaret's story, you're offered a sweeping, bird's-eye view of the whole territory of intimacy and a hopeful statement about achieving one of our basic goals: learning to be more comfortable with who you are.

Margaret says that her promiscuity in her drinking days was the biggest secret of her life. "I've been the headmaster of a high-class girl's school for fifteen years," she says, "and sober for the past five years. Even when I drank I managed to keep up appearances, though. In fact, I was fanatic about it. I tried to be the model professional woman: efficient, nurturing, and, above all, *tailored*." Margaret smiles. "Not a stitch out of place outside, but not a stitch in place *inside*. The stamina it took to get through the day with the horrendous hangovers I had! Now that I'm sober, I can't imagine how I did it."

Margaret says that although her five years of sobriety have been in many ways wonderful—"I feel so much more alive than I used to"—they've also been painful. "I can't get away anymore from the feeling that there's a hole in the center of me, a huge demanding hunger. I guess I'm aware of it now not only because I'm not blitzed on booze anymore but because I'm not *filling* that hunger the way I used to when I drank. Which means, basically, I'm not picking up men anymore."

"I didn't realize how hooked to alcohol my sexual life was until I stopped drinking. I'd had a few reasonably reliable lovers, men I could call up at short notice, usually from a bar after I'd had about four martinis, who would go to bed with me. They say women are supposed to be more emotional about sex than men, but, to tell you the truth, I thought of these men like food. It was like I'd get hungry for them and I'd dial take-out. It didn't matter to me whether or not I loved them or they loved me. I just needed, so desperately needed, intimate contact with *somebody*. I needed to be in someone's arms, feel a man's sexual need for me. It was my means of validating myself, I guess. I was in my late forties back then. I stopped drinking when I was fifty years old, and I was starting to hate the way I looked when I'd pass a mirror. I was beginning to bloat up. Those tailored suits I wore at school had to be let out more and more those last years. I'd do anything to deny the fact that I was a middle-aged woman, and not a terribly attractive one either. Men were my fix, just like martinis were. They could at least temporarily blot out how awful I felt about myself, how fearful . . . "

Margaret had been married in her twenties to a man who matched her drink for drink. "It was the real reason I married him," she says. "He was like a big overgrown playmate who could drink as much as I could. We played at having cocktail parties, going out to restaurants, which were really just excuses to drink. We were like two kids pretending to be grown-ups. Both of us had come from very restrictive nondrinking religious families, and I guess we just wanted to let loose." Margaret and her husband eventually got divorced when, after about ten years of marriage, they decided they weren't having "fun" anymore. Margaret had already begun taking lovers and suspected her husband was doing the same thing. "Playtime was over. The divorce wasn't that painful, really. We just wanted to be free of each other; we'd had enough." Emotional intimacy wasn't something Margaret had really ever known in any relationship, certainly not during her drinking days. "I'd sometimes have huge crushes on this or that man, but after the conquest of going to bed with him, it would always fade. Sometimes

I think I'm just constitutionally incapable of intimacy with anyone. But—the *hunger* . . . "

Margaret tries to explain what she means by hunger. "After all those days when I drank, when I'd avoid looking at myself in any way, even in the mirror, now it seems I can't help *staring* at myself. And I see this sort of desperate look in my eyes. All I'm conscious of sometimes is that *I want something I don't have.* At first I thought it was sex. Would I be able to go home with the same couple of men I used to call up from the bars now that I was sober? Shortly after I stopped drinking, I dialed this one guy, Hank, who had always been at my beck and call. It was terrible. I realized I'd never called him sober before! We had the most awkward conversation. I think I actually talked about the weather. The sound of his voice made me envision his messy apartment and the hangovers I'd have there when I'd wake up at dawn, the alarm clock blasting my brain, so that I could stumble out and get to work. I felt this wave of revulsion. I didn't want to see Hank. I didn't want to see any of my drunken paramours. That wasn't the answer right now."

Margaret began to pour energy into taking better physical care of herself. "I thought maybe that would be healing. I was hearing in AA all the time that sobriety meant doing 'first things first,' and the first thing for me seemed to be that I was overweight and out of shape. So, with the same zeal I used to drink with, I started a crash diet and I joined a gym." In less than a year, Margaret lost forty pounds and was the envy of her colleagues at school and her friends at AA. "I loved that kind of attention, but the pleasure I got out of it was so fleeting. Okay, so I can wear a size four! All that's really happened is that I've turned into a compulsive calorie-counter, and when I miss a day at the gym, I've found a whole new set of reasons to beat myself up." More telling, Margaret says, was that "when I looked into the mirror, the hungry look was still there. And something else now. Fear.

"Fear of letting go, I think. I realize that that wave of revulsion I'd felt when I called up Hank after I got sober wasn't just against Hank. It was just as much against myself. As often as I'd heard in AA that I had to forgive myself and trust in a Higher Power, turn my life over, all of that, there was some part in the center of me as clenched as a fist. I began to see that what I was afraid of was that if I allowed myself to feel any real pleasure, it would be like taking a drink: I wouldn't be able to control myself, I'd go over the edge, I'd lose my mind. Give me an inch, I'll take a mile. My God! It became so clear to me all of a sudden that this was a major reason I drank. Drinking was the only thing I knew how to do to make me lose this terrible sense that all pleasure was self-indulgent. It was the only way I knew how to let go and not *worry* about letting go. I've been so afraid that if I ever really tried to feed this hunger inside me, I'd just capsize, lose control forever."

What Margaret began to realize, however, was that her hunger was beginning to capsize her anyway. "Now that I've got this new svelte body, the whole idea of connecting sexually has come back with huge force. It's like this rush of a river I've got to dam myself up against. But I can't dam myself up against it anymore. I actually gave my phone number to this cab driver the other day, a man who said he liked the way I looked in my dress. I'm obviously chomping at the bit! You don't know how powerful this is. It's like, now that I'm putting so much effort into looking good, I resent any man who doesn't pay attention to me, even a stranger in the street. I never used to look back at men after I walked by them. Now I'll stop and pretend to look in a store window and glance back to see if they're looking back at me. And when a man *doesn't* turn around, I feel like shooting him. How dare he ignore me!"

Margaret shakes her head. "These feelings turn me into a nut case. But as much as this hunger rules me, I still haven't been able to actually move from the feeling to acting on it, to having sex with a man again. And here's where it gets really painful." Margaret connects it to her feelings of revulsion. "I'd remember the most humiliating times. The *shame*," she says. "Like when I was so drunk once I urinated in bed with a man. Or, another time, I did a striptease in front of Hank's roommate, taunting him to join us . . . In fact, one experience was so humiliating and horrible, it became my bottom. The last man I picked up at a bar and went home with actually threw me out. I was blitzed out of my mind and I guess he was too. He couldn't function sexually, and I remember just losing it, railing at him for being a lousy lover. He called me a disgusting whore." Margaret shudders. "It's like as much as I wanted intimate contact with a man—and the urge was overwhelming—the associations about the actual sex would quickly turn nightmarish. I was blocked, horribly, in the center of me. Craving something that kept turning ugly and awful. If the world only knew what a man-hungry immoral whore I was! Even in sobriety I was still really, deep down, just as bad as that last man said I was."

Margaret finally hit what she calls an "emotional bottom" about this. "The dam broke after I met this man, Larry, who had just become a teacher at a boy's prep school affiliated with the school I run. I felt something when I met him I hadn't remembered ever feeling before. I was simply *interested* in him in a way I'd never experienced. He was attractive, funny, articulate, and, in this kind of indefinable way, *good*. There was a sweetness about him. I couldn't imagine him ever being nasty

14

or selfish or lustful in the ways I still thought of myself. He asked me out, and it was the most excruciating date of my life. I was tense and nervous and full of self-hate, at one moment trying desperately to say what I thought he wanted me to say, at the next wishing with all my heart that I could just get up and leave. Finally, pleading a headache, that's exactly what I did. Right in the middle of dinner! I felt like an ass. But I couldn't stand it. He was too perfect. I know that sounds strange. But being with a man who I realized might actually be *good* for me just completely threw me. I wasn't good enough for him. That's what it felt like. I felt this strange, awful mess of being frozen in his presence and yet desperately wanting him to think well of me."

When Margaret got home—"Larry had already left me a message on my answering machine saying he hoped I was all right"—she burst into tears. "I have never felt such self-hate," she says. "What was *wrong* with me? Here I was actually being offered a relationship with a decent, attractive, delightful man, something I'd told myself I'd wanted all my life, and I couldn't take it. I couldn't say yes to it. I realized, painfully, that I had no one in my life I could talk to about any of this, and yet I felt the desperate need to talk to somebody. Luckily I did have a sponsor, even if I'd never used her for anything like an emergency before. But this was an emergency, an emotional emergency in some ways as urgent as the realization I'd had years before when I knew I wanted to stop drinking. Now all I knew was I wanted to stop hating myself . . . "

Margaret dialed her sponsor, got her on the line, and, as she puts it, "blubbered. I can't imagine that much of what I said was intelligible, but it all came out. Big snatches of things. Confessions about my sexual past when I drank, about my fantasies and desires and fears right now in sobriety. A great huge chunk of memory seemed to come out of nowhere about my mother telling me, when I was a little girl, that it was too bad I wasn't pretty, since that's all men cared about. Resentments against my ex-husband for being a baby, for never having really loved me. Love? What did that mean? What was *expected* of me in love? Why was I running away from Larry? Suddenly I hated Larry for being so perfect. It all came out . . . "

An Ordinary Date

Margaret says that her outpouring didn't immediately lead to feeling better: "I felt like a dishrag when I finally ended my conversation with my sponsor. I guess there was relief, but it was the relief of utter emotional exhaustion. I didn't feel wonderful about myself all of a sudden, just completely spent, like a flattened balloon. But the next morning, something lifted. I still can't exactly explain what. I just didn't feel so anxious anymore. I even wanted to talk to Larry again. Maybe just invite him over for coffee."

Later that morning Margaret called Larry and apologized for leaving so abruptly the night before. "Larry seemed relieved that I was feeling better and that he hadn't done something to upset me. It always amazes me to find out once again that other people are as concerned about themselves as I'm concerned about me. Sometimes I think we're all like spinning tops, imagining that the eyes of the world are on our every turn, not realizing that everyone else is spinning in their own orbits thinking the same thing! Anyway, I just felt different about seeing Larry again. I don't know why. It was like some mainspring in me had relaxed."

When Larry came over the next day, however, Margaret had regained some of her old anxiety. "It was a reflex," Margaret says. "When I drank, I never invited a man up to my apartment without expecting it to lead to sex. I clenched when the buzzer rang. I felt the strongest urge for a drink I think I've ever felt in sobriety." But when she let Larry in, Margaret felt a little better. "He just seemed so unthreatening! Whatever had been let loose in me the night before when I blubbered on to my sponsor, it seemed to relax me a little now, allowing me to *see* the world around me a little more clearly. Larry was a nice guy. He wasn't going to try to coerce me into bed. He didn't look like he had an agenda at all . . . "

Margaret poured them both a cup of coffee and they sat down on her couch. "We talked. Work gossip, school stuff. We laughed about colleagues we both knew, especially this one headmaster we both agreed was a pompous ass. At one point, to stress a point, he reached out and touched my hand. And he left his hand on top of mine, even after he stopped talking." Margaret blushes. "I felt like a sixteen-year-old girl. I think I even looked down at my feet shyly, like something out of an Andy Hardy movie. His voice softened. He told me how much he liked me, how much he enjoyed being with me. I mumbled a thank you. He stroked my hand, and I found myself returning the pressure. It had been so long since I'd felt such pure warm affection from anyone! I felt like crying. But then my mind clamped down. The old fears flooded in. Suddenly a voice inside me screamed: 'You're a middle-aged woman. You don't really think he's attracted to you, do you? Or if he is, he probably has some fixation on older women, some fetish about wrinkles! A mother fixation, that must be it!' Suddenly I felt so terribly uncomfortable: hyperaware of a callous in his palm, the slight perspiration that had started on my brow, on my arms. When would all this come crashing down? I was almost *too* aware of the lighting in the room, it was too low, too obviously romantic. Did he think I was trying to seduce *him*? Was

I? It was like part of me slipped out and hovered above, clinically, with no emotion, criticizing every detail. The other part, down there on the couch with Larry, felt awkward and clumsy and too awake, too aware, frozen. Memories of Hank's clumsy, drunken lovemaking suddenly intruded: the smell of stale booze, stale sweat, a vision of gray sheets pulled from the bed, clothes all over the floor . . . It was like some awful monster had invaded my brain, souring everything. I withdrew my hand from Larry's hand. He drew himself up, almost as if he were afraid.

"He said he was sorry. He didn't want me to think he was trying to 'make a move.' He just wanted me to know how much he liked me. Did I want him to leave? Or did I want to go anywhere, take a walk? He was so solicitous. The monster inside me began to quiet down. That hypercritical part of me hovering above seemed to come down and reenter my body. What was happening here? I was simply sitting on the couch talking with a very nice man and drinking a cup of coffee! Suddenly the absurdity of my own feelings, of my own fear, struck me as funny. I laughed. Larry looked perplexed. 'Don't mind me,' I told him. 'I just haven't met a nice guy in a long time.' He seemed to understand. He didn't say anything, but he did return his hand to mine. Then we started talking again, this time about ourselves, about our pasts. He'd been married before too. He told me something about his own fears of getting involved again. It was just a nice talk, that's all. He left after about an hour. We agreed to see each other again for dinner next week. He didn't even kiss me! And that was fine. It was such an extraordinary feeling just to allow myself to *be* with someone in a kind of calm, normal way. It was the biggest revelation I'd had about myself since I'd stopped drinking. I could be normal! Just sit there talking with a man and then say good-bye. I remember thinking to myself, just before he got up to leave, 'I'm doing it!' like I remember saying to myself as a little girl the first time I managed to ride a two-wheel bike. Being with Larry had a kind of reality, manageableness, and closeness that felt completely new to me. It was like I'd stumbled into new territory: I was actually relating to somebody in real life!"

AND DOWN AGAIN: SELF-HONESTY IN THE DAYLIGHT

Unfortunately, this feeling of peace and acceptance didn't last long. Margaret said she wasn't prepared for the flood of feelings, self-questioning, and self-criticism that deluged her later that night and the next morning. "Part of me was laughing. I mean, I was replaying every moment of being with Larry and all we'd done was sit, talk, hold hands, and have a cup of coffee! You'd have thought it was Madame Bovary after she first took a lover! I couldn't help replaying every word, breath, smell, touch, taste—all in a magnified state. Suddenly I was five years down the road: Would he still love me after we got married? Would he start to see other women? Then I'd careen back to now: Does he think I'm too easy? Was he really happy to be with me or just going through the motions? What did the experience *mean* to him? Am I still really just after sex, like I used to be? Is he? Who are we kidding?"

Margaret said her thoughts attacked her like bees. She was exhausted by them. "Everything I thought and felt seemed to contradict itself. I guess what I ended up realizing is that I couldn't *compartmentalize* my feelings the way I used to be able to when I drank. Before, sex was sex and rarely intruded on emotion. Sex, in fact, was always a part of getting drunk, a kind of seamless experience that concluded itself as I slept it off. That was the phrase: I slept it all off; it sloughed off me, like the temporary satiation of a hunger. When the hunger came back, I went through the same motions all over again, the only motions I knew—picked up a man, got drunk, went to bed—and the rut deepened."

But this, Margaret says, was different. There were sensations this time she never remembered feeling before, some good, some bad. She experienced a new emotional reality, a kind of open-endedness. The pressing question "What does it all mean?" was partly the product of her anxiety at going through an experience that *felt* so open-ended. It wasn't the most miraculous moment of her life; neither had it been the most terrible. ("All we did was talk and hold hands and drink coffee!" she kept reminding herself.) *It simply was what it was.* This was profoundly new territory. The prospect of romance or intimacy with a man, the possibility of sex, had always been something so shrouded in mystery, in taboos, in shame, in alcohol, in fantasy, in the dark; and here she was, out in the open—that's what it felt like—facing the possibility of "romance" in broad daylight. This was new and baffling, not least because it was an experience that gave Margaret a glimmer of the discovery that she had a *choice*: the choice to accept rather than judge, hate, or run away from her own feelings. Exercising that choice wasn't easy. It required something of her she'd never been able to do before sobriety: a clearheaded acknowledgment of *how she really felt*, self-honesty in the daylight. It also meant understanding that her feelings might change, that fears might return and fade and return and fade again. "I've accepted for some time in the rest of my life that 'it will pass,' like they say in AA," Margaret says. "But somehow, until now, I never realized that my romantic and sexual feelings might come and go, intensify and fade, in the same way. Why should that be such a surprise? Why did I think sex and intimacy were exempt from the same emotional, changing reality that affects the rest of my life?"

The process of acknowledging and accepting our feelings, all of them, good and bad, is one we need to look at further. Hiram will help us.

THE SLOW JOURNEY FROM SELF-LOATHING TO SELF-ACCEPTANCE

Hiram, with three years free from drugs and alcohol, still feels like he's not sure what planet he's on. "Sometimes I think too much has happened, more than I can handle, in these past few years. But then I keep hearing that God doesn't give us more than we can handle. And, after all, I haven't had a drink through all this time, so maybe that's true. Amazingly, like that Sondheim song, 'I'm still here.'" At forty-five, Hiram has a teenaged son, an angry ex-wife, and, for the past year and a half, a very active sex life as a single gay man.

"I guess I always knew I was attracted to men, even when I was a kid," Hiram says. "Hell, there's no guessing about it. I *knew* that men did something for me women didn't. But the crushes I had on half the football team were the worst secret imaginable. I clung to the idea that maybe this attraction would just go away. There wasn't a book on abnormal psychology in my small town library I hadn't read. I found a few cold paragraphs here and there about how some people just went through a passing phase of 'sexual inversion.' God knows, in the Cleveland suburb I grew up in, with the rigid, conservative Methodist family I came from, the idea of me being gay would have been enough to have them institutionalize me. Sometimes I think my father would have killed me if he knew. It's the main reason I'm glad he's no longer alive. As a teenager, I prayed every night for this passing phase to pass. It didn't, of course. And I'm sure the net effect of all this is similar to every other closeted gay person's experience. I grew up thinking I had to hide who I was inside at all costs. Revealing my sexuality, or even most of my feelings, would, I was sure, make the whole world hate me. Maybe even kill me."

Hiram married his wife right out of college. "I loved Joyce then and I love her now, but the sexual part was always, frankly, a real chore. I could enjoy sex sometimes, like when I was really relaxed, always after a few joints and a half a six pack of beer, enough to close my eyes and fantasize about a man as I made love to my wife. When I was stoned and drunk, it didn't matter; it just loosened me. The morning after, though, when I remembered what a fake the whole experience had been, I just felt worse about myself." Hiram and Joyce had a son about five years after they got married, and Hiram hoped that becoming a father would somehow be the magical thing that would change him into what he thought of as a "real man." "I don't think there's anyone in the world I love more than Rick, my son. And I love being a father, even if, for so many years, I was a lousy one. But none of that took away my sexual fantasies." Hiram says that if his drinking and drugging hadn't also gotten worse, he'd probably still be trying to live the lie that he was straight. "I resorted more and more to getting high: first, to be able to make love with my wife, and second, because it was the only way I could obliterate how much I hated myself. But it got out of hand. Eventually, by the last couple years of my drinking and drugging, it kept me from having any kind of sexual relationship with Joyce at all. I passed out too much to function. Not that I couldn't function sexually elsewhere. Late at night, on the way to getting blitzed out of my mind, I'd sneak out to parks and gay bars, or I'd call up some hustler in Cleveland. This one guy I met in a park gave me an underground list of available men you could call up for hire night or day. Being blitzed gave me the courage to have sex with men. But all it did to me inside was make me hate myself more."

The division Hiram had always felt between his dark, secret, unlovable gay self and the crumbling facade of straight, responsible family man just intensified. "It got so bad I tried to kill myself," Hiram says. "Drunk and on three or four Quaaludes, I threw myself into the town park's pond in the middle of the night. I liked the drama of killing myself in the middle of the town: Now they'd see what they'd done to me! Unfortunately I hadn't banked on the pond being about two feet deep. All I got was wet." The next day, hung over and at his wit's end, Hiram decided to find a psychiatrist. Through therapy, he heard about Alcoholics Anonymous and Narcotics Anonymous. "My despair was so great it went beyond the whole sexual thing. I don't know how to tell you how complete my self-loathing was. Somehow I kept my job—I was a functionary in an insurance office—kept pretty much to myself, did stuff on automatic, but my home life was a wreck. Joyce knew something was really wrong. My son wasn't talking to me, I was such a drunken mess every night. It clicked that the booze and drugs were really getting out of hand, and by my third AA meeting I felt a real moment of surrender." Hiram shakes his head. "I had no idea then what that first moment of surrender was setting up for me. No idea where the door I was opening would lead."

It led Hiram out of his marriage and into a greater acceptance of himself as a gay man. "Or at least a greater freedom to live like a gay man. I still haven't come anywhere near to complete self-acceptance about this . . . "

"You don't go through a lifetime of thinking that the most central part of you—the sexual, loving part—is evil and then suddenly become able to love yourself," Hiram says. "The idea that sex is 'bad' is just too deeply entrenched in me for me to easily change it. Hell, even if I were straight, my Methodist upbringing would have put a chastity belt on sex. But being gay meant being an abomination. And as much as I hear from my sponsor that I need to give myself permission to be who I am and have my feelings, I'm just not there yet."

Hiram says that sometimes he thinks he's sexually compulsive, that the anonymous sex he has is not only evil, but something he'll never be able to stop doing. "There are Twelve-Step meetings dealing with sex addiction even in Ohio," Hiram says, "and I've gone to several. They make me so uncomfortable. It's like the first AA and NA meetings I went to: all hearing about alcohol and drugs did for me was make me want to go out and get high. When I hear about sex, I want to *have* sex! To tell the truth, I think I went to my first Sex and Love Addicts Anonymous meetings to see if I could meet someone who was as hooked to sex as I was so we could have it with each other nonstop!"

Hiram's venues for sex are still pretty much what they were when he was married and felt he had to hide his sexuality: anonymous, late-night encounters in parks and picking up hustlers. "I'm now living in Cleveland, and a lot of people know I'm gay. My ex-wife has gone into counseling, and she's gotten a little more understanding about what I'm going through, although she's still mad as hell at me. And I've even begun to be able to explain things to my son. He's very confused and hurt about it, and I'm not sure how much he's ready to accept or understand, but at least he's listening. But I feel like such a hypocrite. I mean, I tell my son and my wife and the people I know here who I'm 'out' to all the right things: how important it is to be tolerant of diversity, that you're just as capable of love as a gay person as you are as a straight person, that gay people are good people too. But then I think to myself, *Am* I capable of love, of being 'good,' of being at all 'normal'? It goes way beyond being gay. It's like there's something so rotten in the center of me, it won't ever be able to change . . . "

Hiram has had a number of recent sexual encounters that, he says, "border on the unsafe. Hell," he corrects himself, "they don't 'border' on it at all. Twice I've had sex without a condom. And I knew I was doing it. It was like I was really conscious of it. I wasn't swept away or anything. It was this old voice I'd hear just before I'd pick up a drink: 'Fuck it!' That old cynical voice that told me nothing mattered. Just get what pleasure you could get *now*." Hiram says he is afraid. "I know I've put myself at risk for AIDS. Part of me, that cynical part, almost hopes I get it. Death would be the great release: I could just check out. But another part of me, what I identify as the recovering part of me, really wants to live. Here I've finally found the courage to be who I am more than I was ever able to before; I don't want to screw things up now! I think of this terrible imperious sexual urge I've got as some kind of *disease* that comes over me, makes me blind and deaf and dumb, turns me into someone incapable of communicating with anyone beyond physically grabbing at them . . . "

"It's like sex is out of my control, totally. I know it's made me dangle before the flame, the possibility of getting AIDS, way too close these last few times. And only time will tell about whether I got burned. I remember the last hustler I was with, the guy I last had unsafe sex with. I think of his big easy muscular body, and the lostness in his eyes. And I think, we are all so lost, so vulnerable, so childlike, so hungry for contact. It erodes and exhausts me. Because these bouts of sex are as close to intimacy as I seem to be able to get. There are such gaping holes where whole personalities ought to be. All I'm getting is sex, not a person. It's like it's all I think I deserve. This is deaf, dumb, and blind *grabbing*—mute, aching, hungry couplings, something primitive and completely naked, too naked to withstand the cold air of what comes after you come . . . We are hungry and lost, that's the meat of it, hungry and lost and angry and incomplete."

Hiram shakes his head. "I suspect this is just another kind of blindness. I'm romanticizing my own pain, turning it into something big and dramatic and moving. I need to hear what AA teaches me. First things first. Keep it simple. *Take care of yourself.* I've actually begun going back to those Twelve-Step sex addict meetings, and I'm listening a little differently now. Maybe it might be possible to let up on my self-hate a little. Other people identify when I talk about that rotten core in the center of me, other people who are recovering. Maybe there *is* a way out of this terrible self-loathing."

Toward Self-Forgiveness

We've seen Hiram move to the barest beginnings of clarity about himself in his acknowledgment that "it might be possible to let up on . . . self-hate a little." Obviously you don't have to be gay to be self-hating, much as society seems to have bred homophobia in most of us, whether we're straight or gay.

So many recovering men and women identify with that out-of-control, "Screw it!" attitude that Hiram talks about, that cynical voice that tells you to grab for whatever you can get now, because there's no guarantee of getting anything later. So many of us identify with the thought that, deep down, we don't *deserve* more than what we can get out of a quick fix. Pleasure can only be had on the sly, grabbed in the dark. And yet even this pleasure is essential to us: what else can block out our pain? The "mute, angry, hungry couplings" that result from this sexual stance always seem to leave us feeling incomplete, that, as Hiram puts it, "there are gaping holes where whole personalities ought to be."

Dorothy identifies strongly with this feeling of self-hatred and incompleteness, and yet, unlike Margaret or Hiram, she has no history of promiscuity either before or after she stopped drinking. Her problem, she says, is pretty much the opposite. "I'm twenty-six years old," Dorothy says, "and I've never had sex in my life. I'm terrified of intimacy with anyone. And I feel so incredibly *abnormal.*"

Dorothy says her drug of choice was "pills. I took uppers, mostly. I've always been very driven. Diet pills and uppers just seemed like medication I needed to keep me in line. They gave me what felt like boundless energy. They kept me from sleeping, which I was brought up to think of as a waste of time and a sign of self-indulgence." Dorothy lets out a long, quiet sigh. "My mother was a black violinist who married a pharmacist, my father, who is white. She died when I was sixteen. Some part of me still feels she's breathing down my neck, though. 'Honey,' she'd say when I was a little girl, 'if I can make a living as a black woman playing the violin in this prejudiced country, then you can do anything you want. Follow your star,' she'd tell me, 'and go wherever it takes you.' That sounds very nice, I suppose. And I am grateful that I had parents—well, a mother, anyway—who believed that I could do anything I wanted to. But when she died, my father just shut down and it was like he died too. I'd always felt I had to do back flips to get his attention; now it felt like resuscitating the dead. He just lost all interest in life. I'm still not sure about it, but I think he started taking pills himself. I know sometimes he'd admit that he couldn't sleep without 'help.' The more I think about him, the more he seemed like he went through life sedated. He's a pharmacist, after all, so he could get all the Valium or whatever that he wanted. But we never talked about any of that. We never talked about anything.

"So, with a father who stopped being there for me when my mother died, and the memory of my mother's voice telling me to work like hell to get what I wanted, well, that's when I turned up the juice, started working overtime at everything—school, music lessons—and got hooked on pills to keep me revved. I only stopped because they eventually made me so paranoid. I got to a point about five years ago where I literally couldn't step out my front door or answer the phone when it rang. I knew I couldn't go on. I had a choice: kill myself, or get help. And somehow I managed to dial an 800 number for a drug clinic I found in the yellow pages. I knew at that moment anyway that I didn't want to die. Which was real progress for me.

"A lot has gotten better. The clinic eventually turned me on to NA, and it was the first healing and nurturing I'd ever felt from people. But I still feel I have to prove myself; that hasn't gone away. This comes out mostly in music. I play rehearsal piano for the local ballet company, accompany singers, and teach a few students privately. But I've also got to be the first in line at the supermarket, do more routines at the gym than I did the last time I was there, and keep my weight down to exactly 110 pounds." Dorothy says her compulsive tendencies have, if anything, become even more clear to her since she joined Narcotics Anonymous over five years ago than they were when she took drugs. "And now you're asking me about sex?" She laughs, bitterly. "Sex is about number ninety-two on my list of priorities. I've always had so much else to *do*. Who has time for it?" What isn't far down on the list of her priorities, however, is dealing with a sometimes crippling feeling of loneliness. "I dream about connecting somehow to a soul mate," she says. "Sometimes I'll have private crushes on this or that man. But that's what they are: private. It's like a tap got turned off in me years ago and now it's rusted shut. I say that sex isn't important to me, and it's true: *sex*, on its own, is almost a disgusting idea. All that rolling around naked. The idea of being that physical, that *out of control*, terrifies me. And while I tell myself it doesn't matter, the fact that I don't feel either black or white is somehow symbolic. I don't feel like I'm *anything*. Even my body might be either male or female, at least clothed! I'm very slim, I've got small breasts, my hair is cut short. What race or sex am I anyway? I was in therapy for a couple years, and the woman seemed to think that maybe my fear of sexual and emotional intimacy came from some kind of child abuse. And I think of my quiet, withdrawn father. I'm pretty sure he never 'tampered' with me. I don't think that's it. But he never loved me very much either. So maybe that's a part of the psychological root of all this. In recovery I've learned not to torture myself with self-analysis. 'Just pay attention to now,' I keep hearing at meetings. I try to. But I'm still so locked up. How will I ever be able to connect on more than a polite, superficial level with anybody?

"Then I think, why can't I just get into a close platonic friendship with someone? Someone who can share my interests, my musical life, my mind . . . But no one measures up. Or I don't measure up to whoever it is I've got a secret crush on. And, as much as I say sex isn't the issue, when I let myself fantasize, I'm drawn like a magnet to the bedroom door, and then I freeze. The bedroom door is always locked. I'm afraid to let go emotionally in any way with anybody because I'm sure that I'm going to have to 'deliver the goods' down the line and have to have sex. So I've kept myself tied up in my head, my activities, my busy-ness—and my loneliness. They say sobriety is supposed to be happy, joyous, and free. Sometimes I feel like killing myself. I know *that* isn't what sobriety is supposed to make me feel! But sometimes I feel so stuck, like I'm the only one in the world like me. I'm so embarrassed to tell anyone that I've never had an intimate love relationship. I feel like a freak."

ACKNOWLEDGING THE DAMAGE

Dorothy's perspective got a jolt recently when late one night, flipping through the TV channels, she happened to tune into a National Geographic nature program. She said it was "a typically insomniac night. I was obsessed by the schedule I had the next day, lessons piled on rehearsals and a meeting with my accountant and—I guess this was the real reason for anxiety— a late-afternoon coffee date I'd made with a tenor who wanted to talk to me about doing a recital. That was a business date on the face of it, but I felt the old familiar spark of adoration inside me when I'd met him the previous week. I was already pushing him toward that secret pedestal: I'd found another secret crush. And it had the effect on me all my other secret crushes had always had: it made me want to shut down and hide. So, here I was, after one in the morning, nervously scanning through channels on the TV, when I was stopped short by the sight of a gorilla mother nursing a tiny baby. I like nature shows on TV, so I stopped for a moment and watched."

It was the gorilla mother's expression that Dorothy now realizes riveted her most. "I'd never seen such a half-hearted mother. It was like, 'Well, I guess I have to hold this little thing in my arms and suckle it, but I can't really remember why.' By some kind of reflex, she jostled the baby rhythmically; you couldn't call it rocking, really, it was just jostling. It's like some buried instinct dimly told her that's what you were supposed to do with a baby. The baby clung to her mother's nipple, trying to stay on it, sometimes slipping off from the maternal jostling, then blindly grasping for more nourishment. Mama couldn't have looked more bored. Meanwhile, all these attendants, these animal keepers and scientists and biologists, were all cooing and encouraging mama from outside the cage, trying to get her to pay a little more attention to her daughter. Apparently this mother had had another little baby a couple of years before and got bored with it after a while, left it huddling and crying in the corner of the cage. By the time the attendants got the baby out of the cage, he was too dehydrated to survive. So they were really pulling for mama and baby this time and poised to save the little girl quickly if mama lost interest again . . . "

Although Dorothy didn't exactly know why, she started to cry. "Sure, the whole scene was sad. But I'm not a sentimental person. I don't usually get all mushy and coo-ey about animals. I'm just fascinated by them. But something clicked in me this time, something that went deeper than fascination. I *understood* something. I saw this harried, out-of-focus creature, this gorilla mother pent up behind bars, and I thought, What do they expect? They take an animal out of its natural home, stick it in a cage, subject it to all these strange human beings poking and prodding it, and then expect it to be a perfect mother? Damaged goods. This gorilla mama was one damaged lady. And so was I. Until that moment I'd never allowed myself to feel compassion or forgiveness for being the locked-up person I was. But something about this gorilla being forced to go through the motions to please her keepers. My God! Was there a better description of how I felt in my own life? I was always going through *motions*. Trying desperately to please, to win, to survive. And I started to think of the baby gorilla, poor, senseless little thing. Because her mama was damaged, how could the damage *not* be passed on to her? It turned out the attendants did have to separate her from her uninterested mother. They shot mama with a sedative and grabbed the little baby out of the cage. And now a lot of strange human hands, sounds, and smells were going to bring this baby up. I felt such identification with both these creatures, somewhere beyond words. It was like, yeah, That's it. I'm some sort of different *species* that somehow got into the wrong hands. And I've been trying to pretend I could be black or white or female or asexual or a musician or an athlete or a friend or a . . . How could I even get close to envisioning myself as a lover? Suddenly it became really clear to me that I was so separated from myself, it was no wonder I couldn't imagine letting someone into my life, much less my bed. I was struck by just how enormous the damage in me was. It hit me that I hadn't made contact with *me*, my feelings, who I really was, maybe ever. That's what I had to do. That's what sobriety is about, isn't it? Making contact with yourself first. You can't give what you haven't got. And, despite five years off drugs with some kind of steady program in NA, I still hadn't developed any real faith or trust. I still hadn't relaxed and allowed myself to be me."

Dorothy finally got some sleep, went through the rest of her busy day almost on automatic, and then got to the dreaded appointment with the tenor. "Except," she says, "I wasn't dreading it so much. I don't know what I'd allowed to release in me the night before when I cried over the gorilla show, but I simply didn't feel as tense or apprehensive as I expected to. I was even looking forward to meeting him! This freaked me out. Where was the old, locked-up girl I used to be? I'd *relaxed* a little. And okay, it wasn't some magical, total transformation. I mean, I still had him up there on the pedestal. And I still dragged myself down: he'd find out I wasn't half the musician he was, he would try to let me down easy when he actually heard me play—the whole self-denigration bit I do to myself whenever I get near someone who interests me. But something seemed wrong, out of kilter about all that beating up on myself, all that negative projection. It was like something sort of separated in me. I could begin, for a moment, to disengage from those old negative feelings and voices and see that they didn't have to be me. That was it: I had a choice. I didn't have to stay in the same old self-hating, fearful rut. And it felt freeing. I allowed myself to enjoy being with this singer in a whole new way. We even laughed a lot. Grim little humorless me laughing!"

Since that time, Dorothy has put herself through many of her old paces. "The old dread came back: I was crazy to think this guy might actually like me. The old irrational sexual fears cropped up too. For someone who says she has no interest in sex, it's amazing how quickly I'll imagine what it would be like to be in bed with a man—and how much I'm sure I'd hate it!" But the slight distance Dorothy allowed herself to experience between her reflexive, negative feelings and the more open sense of herself as someone who had a *choice* to get out of her ruts has stayed with her. "It's like some door opened a crack: there's a little light, a little promise of hope where there had been none before. And another amazing thing is I can talk about this stuff! I'm talking right now about it, and it's because I've realized that I won't be shot down by a lightning bolt if I open my mouth and say how scared and unsure I am. My NA meetings have become a whole new source of comfort and release for me. I still don't let a lot of people know I've never had sex with anyone. Some fears die harder than others. But in private, I can talk about it with my sponsor, with people my heart and intuition tell me it will be okay to talk about it. And, Lord, the relief is amazing." Dorothy's face drains of tension; she obviously feels that relief right now. "I don't know how all this will evolve. But the very idea of 'intimacy' doesn't terrify me anymore. Now I'm only nervous about it!"

Dorothy, Margaret, and Hiram are all facing difficult fears about sex in sobriety. Despite the differences in their sexual behavior (or lack thereof), at the core, they are all facing the same fear of allowing who they really are to emerge.

So often the particulars of our lives loom so large that we can't help but feel that they make us unique, that, as Dorothy puts it, we're some separate "species" from everybody else. However, over time, recovery seems to put the lie to this. We allow ourselves to pay more heed to the Twelve-Step suggestion: "Identify, don't compare." The particulars of our lives are the product and confluence of any number of circumstances, details of background and genetics, and chance and fate, all of which provide a kind of covering for the heart, a heart that seems to beat very similarly in all of us.

But these particulars do, of course, still trip us up. And, as we've seen with Margaret, Hiram, and Dorothy, these stumbling blocks can seem to turn into towering walls when we enter the realm of sex. Some ground is gained, as we've seen, when you can begin to acknowledge and articulate some of your fears, first to yourself and then to someone outside yourself. It's like a problem in physics: you learn to give the tension that's built up inside you some kind of satisfying release. Release *isn't* satisfying when it happens unconsciously, when we take no control over the channel the release takes—in other words, when we blindly grab for a pain killer. This unconscious urge to grab for quick, pain-killing release is what characterized most of our drinking and drugging histories.

The impulse to reach for a quick palliative doesn't always go away after we've quit drinking or drugging. Sometimes the urge manifests, as it still sometimes does with Hiram, in blind, grasping, anonymous encounters. Sometimes, as with Margaret, the palliative resides in pouring energy into desperate self-improvement: counting calories, overexercising, turning yourself into some imagined perfect being (the attainment of which, of course, is always just out of reach). And sometimes, oddly, it can come, as it has with Dorothy, not only from driving yourself physically, but also in beating yourself up for your inadequacies! This may seem like an odd way to seek release, but it is a very common one for recovering people. We learn, sometimes, to take refuge in what we *can't* do, which becomes its own kind of release, a way we can excuse ourselves for why we don't feel capable of doing anything better. ("Of course I drink," says the nonrecovering alcoholic. "I'm a drunk. What do you expect?")

But these reflexive releases aren't very effective. The pain is still there—always. The solution is to find ways to address that pain more consciously. As Margaret, Hiram, and Dorothy become more conscious of what their real fears and negative assumptions are, they each experience a feeling of choice, a widening of options. Not that this initial more spacious glimpse of alternative feelings and actions is a magical cure-all. Part of learning to be honest with yourself involves developing an increasing respect for how deep the damage goes. It takes more than a little light to illuminate this damage at its source.

We discover the need for this light when we come face to face with our desires. For many of us, our desires—and especially our sexual desires—feel wrong or bad. We take them as evidence of our weakness and self-indulgence. Our very fantasies, we believe, border on the sick or the silly, branding us as separate, maybe even abnormal. The bottom line is: whatever our sexual feelings are, somehow they're automatically wrong. What's more, it's our fault. If only we were better people, we'd experience all that exalted love that religion and parents and romance novelists tell us we're supposed to be feeling. But what we really feel like, to tell the truth (although we find this awfully hard to do with ourselves or with anyone), is as far from that angelic stuff as a worm is from the moon.

The assumption that our sexual selves are, almost by definition, "bad" is one commonly made by recovering people, and it's one few of us have the willingness to meet head on. It produces a kind of Jekyll and Hyde split in us that can sour even our happiest moments in sobriety. Let's allow ourselves to invite Dr. Jekyll and Mr. Hyde into the same space. The first surprise you'll have is discovering that they've already met (however privately). The bigger surprise is that they can turn into very good friends.

CHAPTER 3

The Jekyll and Hyde Split

If you've ever "made a searching and fearless moral inventory" of yourself (completed a fourth Step), you've undoubtedly had to face a range of uncomfortable memories and feelings, probably the most debilitating of which is shame. No human being seems to be devoid of shame, even if consciousness of it may be very deeply buried. Often it's tied to the first messages we got from our parents about sex, our bodies, how we should or shouldn't express our anger or sadness or joy. The net effect is that we come to believe that there are facts about us that are simultaneously disgusting *and* unchangeable. Some of the more obvious "facts" (which we'll explore in more depth in chapter 5) may be purely physical: you've decided that you're abnormally under- or overendowed in this or that crucial area; you're doomed to kinky hair, baldness, shortness, the wrong skin color, and so forth. Other sources of shame may have to do with background, as when you feel you've had inadequate parents, schooling, or friends or are of the wrong ethnic, economic, or social status. Even deeper, you may be convinced you're turned on by the wrong things, that your fantasies or sexual preference are abnormal. In every case you damn yourself for not being able to change something that you're equally convinced *must* change for you to be acceptable. Shame creates an impossible situation: we're stuck being something we can't tolerate being. Unfortunately, feelings of shame run so deep and are so humiliating to most of us that we freeze at the very prospect of exploring them. Often, when someone close to us gets too near these areas, we get defensive and lash out or withdraw. We protect ourselves. We blame or defend or isolate.

Recovering alcoholics and addicts commonly experience an exaggerated fear of traveling this territory: we're not only dealing with childhood roots of shame, we're usually trying to come to terms with the havoc we've wreaked as adults, drunk and high and out of control. I haven't met a recovering alcoholic or addict yet who hasn't felt the urge to flee these feelings. Doing a fourth Step, for most of us, requires taking a very courageous leap indeed.

Is it possible to counter these debilitating fears and move beyond them to some kind of freedom and serenity?

Yes. But this requires facing and defining exactly what your fears *are*. Let's look at a number of people who've managed to do exactly that.

THE UNNERVING EXPERIENCE OF KINDNESS

Ian, a thirty-seven-year-old Londoner with four years in Alcoholics Anonymous, says, "I think my fear is based on self-hate. I'm terrified to face the true, rotten person I seem to be convinced I am. Even the idea of allowing myself to feel or face certain memories—dropping my trousers in the middle of a party once, trying to get an orgy going while bombed out of my mind, and a lot worse—puts me in contact with a whole half of myself that feels hateful, sinful, *evil*. Until recently, the best I've been able to do in sobriety with this half of me, what I think of as my Hyde half, is push it down.

"For the first year or so of sobriety, this seemed to work well enough. I was able to keep this monstrous Hyde part of me in check by white-knuckling it. Whenever I had the urge, for example, to call up a prostitute, which I used to do frequently and without thinking when I drank, I'd call my sponsor instead. I just kept pushing this evil self down again and again. But after a while I couldn't do that anymore; it stopped working. This Hyde half of me turned out to be far more powerful than I ever realized. It started to come roaring up again. In my second year of sobriety, I just gave in to it. I began calling the old numbers, going out with whores again, lying to my friends and sponsor about where I went on weekend nights."

Ian shakes his head angrily. "I would get so angry at myself. Sometimes I still do. *Why* haven't I gotten completely, spiritually, mentally, attitudinally *cured* yet? Even sober, I'm not sober! What will it take? Do I need to join some monastery? Have myself committed, locked up? The worst part of it is that the Jekyll half of me—the nice, responsible, sober, kind, reliable half of me—seems like more and more of a sham, just as it used to when I drank and tried to cover it up, tried to look like a decent human being. The Hyde half turns out to be more than a half. I'm beginning to think it's the real me. Certainly when I'm in the dark, taking off a strange woman's clothes, feeling her hands on my body, that's when I'm feeling my *real* self, if you want the truth. Not when I'm pouring coffee at an AA meeting! It's like the whole life I live out in public is a sham, a pretense, a put-on. Which is exactly what it felt like when I drank."

Ian says that the harder he has tried to work his program in AA, "sometimes it just seems to provoke Hyde more, make that part of me even stronger! Up until recently, when I've tried to do an inventory about my sex life or ask God for strength to deal with it, all it seems to end up doing is make me want to go out and *have* sex. It's a bit like the first few times I went to AA meetings, before I stopped drinking. I'd known for years that my life was out of control, that I was an alcoholic, that things were a mess, but I couldn't surrender to this. I just couldn't make it to the first Step. All hearing about alcohol made me want to do is go out and drink. I heard somewhere that the unconscious mind admits no negatives: when you tell it 'Don't drink,' all it hears is the 'drink' part. That's what went on with me, anyway. I'd leave the meeting early and find the nearest bar and get bombed. And usually end up in some pickup or prostitute's bed to sleep it off . . . " Ian finally was able to surrender to his alcoholism after one of these post-AA meeting debauches. "I woke up in some strange bed. I had no idea where I was, who I was with, what had happened the night before. Oddly, the woman next to me turned out to be attractive, and she was very sweet to me when I finally came to. She offered me breakfast. She was so damned *nice*. Somehow this just made me feel worse. It would have been better if she'd been a screaming harridan who threw me out. Then I would have got what I deserved! Who was this nice woman? Why was she treating me so kindly? I felt bewildered. Some new feeling began to seep in, crowding out the usual self-loathing. It was a dual feeling, really. Clarity and a little bit of hope. Clarity beyond realizing I was a drunk. I'd known that for years. It was a clarity that told me I could get help if I stopped drinking, even that I was *worth* helping. Which is how the hope came in. Some sea change had occurred. I got a glimpse that there were alternatives to the rut I was in."

The unnerving experience of kindness: that was what bewildered Ian the most. "When I went back to AA, I began to see that kindness, unconditional love really, had always been there for the taking. People actually cared about whether I stayed sober, whether I felt good about myself or not. I'd never been able to *register* this caring before. Something about that woman I woke up with tipped the scales. I often wonder whatever became of her. I never saw her again. But she opened a door for me. She opened it with what still seems to me to be totally undeserved tenderness, kindness . . . "

However, believing that he *deserved* love and kindness, that he had the choice to take a tack of self-acceptance rather than self-hate, has turned out to be the most difficult task Ian says he's faced in sobriety. "Now that the pink-cloud gratitude I felt in the first year or so of sobriety has lifted and I have a clearer view of the rubble of my personality, well, the old self-hate has roared back up with a vengeance. I know intellectually that this is at the root of why I seek release in the old dark sexual escapades. It's gotten compulsive. I really don't feel I've got the power to stop myself from calling up yet another whore. And, Lord, now that you can charge these women on credit cards, the debt has become overwhelming. Whatever tiny gleam of liking myself I once was capable of has been stamped out. Now I'm like some creature, always looking for the next lay. An animal really. It's amazing I haven't picked up a drink again. Somehow that commitment has stayed fast throughout all of this. But I can't be sure it always will."

Recently, Ian went through a long day and night of feeling especially out of control. He took the day off from his office job, bought some pornography that he spent the morning "slavering over," then began calling numbers of escort services listed at the back of the magazines. Ultimately, he had sex, or attempted to have sex, with three women ("the first one made 'out calls' and came over to my apartment; the second two were in a brothel I'd been to before"). He felt, he says, "battered into submission. It was clear, clear as it had never been before, that I wasn't even after sex anymore. To put it politely, I could barely function with the second woman and was completely useless with the third. They didn't care, they were getting their money. But I was a physical and emotional dishrag. I somehow came to in the stained sheets of this ratty bed—the third woman vainly attempting to arouse me through a variety of passionless mechanical means—and suddenly I saw myself and the whole scene as if for the first time. It all struck me as absurd. What on earth was I trying to do? What was I after? It clearly wasn't sex. I hadn't, at that point, the least interest in sex. And yet I kept forcing myself to keep trying to have it anyway. What was going on?"

What interested Ian most was that this moment of revelation wasn't accompanied by the usual self-hatred. "It was more a feeling of deep fascination, strong *curiosity*, really. It was a little like how I felt when I'd stopped smoking. I'd managed to put down cigarettes two years before, after two years in AA. What happened at the moment I decided to quit was much like what was happening now, in this ratty whorehouse bed. Some part of me sort of detached, floated up, and looked down at the mechanics going on below and found it all absurd. *I didn't want to do it anymore.* That was what I felt; that was the real moment of revelation. It was like my epiphany about being an alcoholic: I didn't want to drink anymore. Not: 'I should stop drinking because it's bad for me.' It was a genuine desire for sobriety. It wasn't negative; it wasn't depriving me of anything. It was *giving* me something." Ian extracted himself from his day- and night-long debauch with very different feelings than he was used to after such debauches. These feelings were in fact so different, so strangely unthreatening that he even wanted to share them with his sponsor. "I'd assiduously avoided mentioning anything about sex with my sponsor past a very general statement of confusion. Yes, I'd done a fourth Step and was fairly explicit about sex in it, but I never mentioned anything I'd done in sobriety. It was all a list of the stuff I did when I drank. Up to now I'd kept whole areas of my sober life to myself. They were just too shameful to tell anyone about. But something about the discovery I'd made, that the problem really wasn't 'sex' at all, made me feel more able to talk about it. It didn't seem so evil, somehow. I saw it less judgmentally, more compassionately."

Ian found himself talking to his sponsor more openly than he ever had before. And, he says, "it opened up that kindness again. The kindness I'd first received from that woman, so long before, on the morning after my last drink when I woke up and felt my first ray of hope. The kindness I depended on in the early days and weeks of sobriety. My sponsor didn't judge me. He seemed genuinely interested in the insights I'd had about sex meaning something other than sex. He even shared some of his own, similar experiences with me. But the biggest thing he focused on was my statement that *I felt most myself* when I was in the midst of the darkest sexual experience. That interested him the most. He told me there was a key there that I might want to think about."

THE MYTH OF THE "DARK" HALF

Ian's sponsor suggested that the only thing that kept Ian's "dark half" dark was his resistance to turning on the light.

"The darkness could always be illuminated. Things were only dark if we kept them that way, which I'd been doing for years out of fear. But it's an area that cries out for exploration! In this dark part of me is a crucial part of who I really am. I felt most like myself in these forbidden areas because these were the areas where I let my guard down, where I allowed my inhibitions to lift, where, truly, I didn't *care* about how I was coming across to the world. Most importantly, it was where I didn't feel judged. Paying someone to have sex means you're in control. You can get them to do what you want them to do. They won't judge you. They'll let you be who you are. It's part of their job, really, to accept you! Is it any surprise I felt most like myself in such encounters? But the big news for me was that this realm wasn't something to hate. This part of me I'd labeled Hyde wasn't some monstrous, evil aberration. It was the expression of a very primal, important need in me: the need to be myself, including my sexual self, without censure. The need to make intimate contact with someone. It was a very *precious* part of me, which on some level I must have known or I wouldn't have gone to such lengths to protect it, to keep it away from the world's judgment, even from what I projected would be my sponsor's judgment. Really, in some ways this dark Hyde part was the *most* precious part of me! It was the most naked me: who I was in secret. Who I was to *myself*." Ian says he's begun to see that every time he dismisses his sexual urges with a negative label, he's depriving himself of an opportunity to understand more about what these "urges" may really be encouraging him to seek. "I saw, at the moment when I was still trying to have sex even though, physically, I truly didn't want to, that whatever contact or freedom or release I was after had to do with something different from and deeper than sex. And in that one extraordinary moment, I didn't judge myself. I *accepted* my hunger; I didn't hate it. It was the first glimpse of relief, of freedom about all this, I've ever felt. And a lasting effect is of having let in that same unnerving feeling of kindness I felt from other people when I began to get sober. Only now I'm learning I can give that kindness to myself."

How this translates into behavior is something Ian is very much still in the process of working out. "In America you've got all these Twelve-Step programs dealing with sex and love addiction or compulsion. You won't find a lot of those groups in England. Good Lord, it's still something of a stigma to go to a psychotherapist in England; even AA is regarded with suspicion! I was brought up to think of all this as self-indulgent navel-gazing. But there are a couple of self-help groups in London I've investigated, and they've helped me to some degree to look at this sexual compulsion business in a new light. I suppose what I'm learning, as I listen to other people grappling with their own sexual demons, is something I've known all along, something that my alcoholism has taught me. Compulsion—the urge to repeat a behavior again and again, despite incontrovertible evidence that it's not giving you what you want—seems to happen when what I call the 'spirit' rams up against fear. It's like, here's this river trying to rush up against a dam, a dam that just gets bigger and bigger the more the river pushes against it. More and more water rushes in, the dam gets bigger and bigger, and after a while, the dam and water start to fill the landscape, taking everything over completely. The obvious solution seems to be to dismantle the dam so that the water can flow through and find its level, its natural banks. But, out of fear, we keep building the dam higher. It's this *resistance* that traps us and that keeps the dynamic going, stronger and more urgently than ever. That urgency is the spirit trying to get through and find its natural flow. Compulsion is the product of *fighting* the natural flow of things.

"I know I'm not the only human being in the world—God knows, not the only person in England!—who sees his own sexuality as evil, something to build up dams against. I think a lot of why I drank was sort of to play in the water on the other side of that dam, to have sex without guilt. Alcohol could usually wash away enough inhibitions to *allow* me to play in these dark waters. But it eventually eroded everything else in my personality too. I was playing in these secret dark waters at the expense, finally, of my life. When I got sober, it was because I allowed the dam that alcohol had created to dismantle, to let the flow of my being go where it would without the resistance alcohol put up. And I'm beginning to see that maybe the same thing could happen with sex. It's a matter of introducing the dark half to the light half, of allowing both to exist and flow into each other, really. What I'm slowly finding is that maybe I'm *not* this terrible divided self after all."

Ian feels at the very beginning of this new chapter of recovery. "I still don't feel good enough about myself to imagine having a sexual relationship with someone nice. For so many years the only way I could imagine anyone having sex with me was if I tricked them into it or paid them for it. But now there's at least the glimmer of possibility that I could learn to feel differently about all this. And this feeling of hope comes from accepting who I am, not resisting it. Maybe I *don't* have to see my self as divided. That faint hope is about as much as I've been able to come up with so far, but it's a start, and maybe not a bad one."

FACING PAIN, SADNESS, AND RAGE: PART
OF THE BEAUTY

More than six thousand miles away, in a very different culture and with a very different background, Carolyn is dealing with some of the same issues Ian faces about his "divided self." Carolyn waits tables part-time in a coffee shop in Seattle. Once she was "royally hooked to prescription pain killers and cheap wine. I got so I could turn into a zombie on cue, blocking out anything I didn't feel like facing, which was pretty much everything." Now, at thirty-nine, she's in her sixth year of sobriety in AA and NA. "So much has changed and gotten better," she says. "I'm married, for one thing. Stan and I have a child, Susannah, who just had her second birthday. Changing from the paranoid, blotto wreck I was to a married woman and mother who's holding down a job, well, you can't know what a miracle that is."

Carolyn met Stan in an NA meeting. "Stan is different from any man I've ever been involved with before, and not only because he was the first sober man of the bunch. He's just not the kind of low-class bum I used to get hooked up with. Not that there were that many men before Stan. I wasn't easy or anything. Even when I was drunk and zonked on pills I wouldn't go home with just anybody. But they were greasers, most of them. Motorcycle type guys, jeans and torn T-shirts, tough, silent, and either drunk or hung over." Carolyn shakes her head in disgust. "I don't miss them. They were macho brutes—silent, stupid men, just like my father, most of them. Never cared much for me, beyond me being their lady, cooking for them, going to bed with them. First man I moved in with, I was eighteen. The rest—there were four more live-in relationships—followed the same model. I was there as a fixture, something to take care of their needs. You wanna know the truth? I hated those guys. There were times, still drunk after a long night of putting up with Bill or Jack or Andy, I'd sit bolt upright in bed, next to one of them snoring away, and seriously consider getting a gun and shooting him. I was either a sex toy or a maid, something they used until they got bored with it. My life, sober, with Stan, and now our little miracle of a daughter Suzie, couldn't be further from all that terrible stuff. The drinking and the fights, the drunken sex . . . " Carolyn seems to deflate. "Of course, that's the problem. I hated those men, but the truth is, I miss how I felt going to bed with them." Carolyn pauses for a moment, frowning. "But that's not really true. So much of sex for me was putting up with a man's desire for it. I don't know that I ever enjoyed it very much while I was doing it. I just find myself fantasizing about the *memory* of it. Some details won't leave me alone. Especially about the first man I lived with, Bill. Bill was the kinkiest man I've ever been with, I guess. He'd send away to Frederick's of Hollywood for black corsets and negligees and fishnet stockings. We'd get drunk and he'd order me to get dressed up. He'd even push me around a little. Sometimes— this is hard to admit, but it's true—he'd even slap me around a little. Not hard. It wouldn't hurt. But it was incredibly exciting. I mean, we'd be drunk and all. He'd never talk about it the next day and neither would I. It was like this secret world we could only enter drunk. After a half gallon of wine, he'd say, 'Get 'em out, Carolyn,' and that would be it, the signal to drag out whatever black lacy things we were into at the moment. And I would. The sex was unbelievably exciting, at least that's how I remember it. He'd be so tough and mean and sullen and silent, and I'd be strutting in front of him in my outrageous outfits making him go crazy. Finally, he'd get up and push me down on the bed, give me a slap on the rear end, maybe . . . "

Carolyn sighs. "I can't get this out of my mind. And I'm suffering for it. So is Stan. The bare truth is, I just don't find my husband attractive. Sometimes I think that's why I chose him. I guess it seemed to me that sobriety was a time to clear everything away, start from an entirely clean slate. I thought I could erase everything, not only my old behavior, but my memories, my sexual thoughts, anything that used to excite me; it all seemed so shameful. I thought I could just sweep that away in the trash. Sure, maybe do a fourth Step on it, make a laundry list of my sins, tell my sponsor about them, but basically get rid of it without thinking too much about it. Go on and be the saintly woman I knew God wanted me to be, that I *could* be now that I wasn't wasted anymore. The only thing that was important to me in sobriety, I thought, was to make a good home and hearth and have a loving family. That's all I wanted. And when I got that, I was sure I'd be perfectly satisfied. Live happily ever after."

This isn't exactly how things have turned out. "We do have a nice home," Carolyn says. "A small ranch home with a fireplace, outside of the city. We're decent to each other. We hardly ever fight, well, at least we didn't used to until recently. But when it comes time to go to bed . . . " Carolyn says she hates the term *frigid*, but she admits it's a pretty accurate word for how she feels in bed with Stan. "Sometimes I want to crawl out of my skin when he touches me," she says. "It's gotten really bad. The very qualities I chose him for—he's gentle, safe, nonthreatening, sweet, considerate—make him an incredible turn-off to me in bed. And I can't stand myself. What's wrong with me? Why can't I like him for who he is? Why do fantasies of Bill keep tormenting me? Memories of how we looked in the ceiling mirror Bill had put up over our bed so we could see every drunken toss and turn? God, sometimes I think, maybe if I got into some of those old Frederick's of Hollywood outfits with Stan I could light some kind of fire. But I'm so ashamed of that part of my past. And I've put on pounds since I got sober. It's like I'm trying to cover that old self up with fat, make it unattractive, make sure I could never get *in* those sexy black negligees. I think I'd freak Stan out of his gourd if I tried. He thought he married this sweet, sober, rational, hardworking woman. Little does he know the sex-hungry monster at the center of me . . . "

When Susannah was born two years before, the pressures and chaos of dealing with an infant allowed Carolyn to ignore some of the dissatisfaction she felt romantically with Stan. "We were just too tired most of the time to think about having sex in those first months, all through the first year, up till recently. But now that Stan's mother is helping out, coming in days to take care of the baby while Stan and I go out to work, now things have let up a little, and when I get home I find I'm facing my husband in a new way. It's like I can't *ignore* him anymore. He sits there like a big fat sweet lump of something. Perfectly nice, patient to a fault, but so unbelievably—*boring*. I'm starting to feel all this anger. It's like, sometimes I don't think he's a real man. He's this big teddy bear. Lately, when it's come time to go to bed with him, I've let him go on ahead and I stay up, making myself read, making myself wait until he's asleep and he won't reach out in that old pathetic, pleading way of his and say, 'Honey, please?' Damned wimp. That's what I'm really thinking. He's a damned wimp. Sometimes I even wish he'd get drunk or something. Go into a rage. Do something wild and terrible. Lose his fat and get lean and mean. Overwhelm me. But he's a physical, mental, and spiritual Pillsbury dough boy."

Carolyn says that she now thinks having a baby was her attempt to "fix our marriage, give us something to hold us together. Something to make up for the passion that was never there to begin with." But Susannah hasn't turned into this panacea. "She's a headstrong girl, just like me," Carolyn says. "And I don't know that I'm so good with her. Oh, there are times I look at her and this incredible feeling of love takes over. I can't believe the miracle of her being my daughter. But there are other times . . . God, this is hard to admit." Carolyn closes her eyes for a moment, then continues softly. "Sometimes I hate Susannah. Like I hate Stan. It's like they're in my life to *hold me back*. Whatever it is I'm in this life to do, it has to be more than being Stan's dutiful wife and Susannah's doting mother. These fantasies of Bill, back in the old days, it's like they're some emblem of a life I still should have, still want to have. I want some passion, some grand excitement. I don't want to be stuck here in a sexless marriage with a demanding baby in some suburban house, waiting tables for food money . . . Sometimes, you know what I want to do? Pick up a bottle of pills and a bottle of wine and have one last fling. Waste myself again and never wake up. My life seems like one big obligation. There's no joy in it. I feel like I'm sinking slowly down into some tar pit, and there's nothing I can do to get up and out of it . . . "

Carolyn has considered taking a lover. "I've flirted with this guy, a mean-looking cuss named Duke who cooks in the restaurant I work in. He's like the men I used to know. He reeks of beer, for one thing. I've started fantasizing about him a lot lately. But I can't do it. First of all, when would I have the time for that? And it makes me feel so guilty, even to think about it. Because, as much as I feel trapped by my little life with Suzie and Stan, they are the only home, the only family I've got. And there's still the sober me, the me who keeps going to AA and NA meetings and talks about her daily problems and reads the literature and tries to do the Steps, the me who wants to have a nice, normal, respectable, above-board life. It's like an angel is talking into one ear, a devil's talking into the other. And they're making me nuts. I'll be at work and start making eyes at Duke and he'll leer back at me and suddenly I'll freak out and think, Oh, I can't wait to get home and have meat loaf and mashed potatoes and sing to little Susannah and watch the evening news with Stan just like a happy normal American family. Then I'll get home and Susannah will be screaming and Stan will sit there looking like a hurt puppy dog and his mother will be nagging at me to get this or that for the baby, and all I want to do is go back to Duke, take off my clothes, and have sex on the restaurant kitchen floor. It's like, wherever I am, I want to be somewhere else. This isn't what sobriety is supposed to be like, is it?"

Carolyn's anger and confusion built up to such a point that she couldn't contain it, either at work or at home. "It's like there was nowhere for this energy to go. I started snapping at customers at the coffee house, real snide and sarcastic—you know, 'Right *away*, sir'—when someone nagged at me for service. My boss started noticing and giving me warnings. And at home, God, I know I was turning into a bitch. I'd order Stan around, and he'd cringe. I know he'd feel like he had to walk on eggshells around me. I was so impatient with Suzie too. When I got pregnant I swore I wouldn't get angry at my baby the way my mother used to get angry at me, but, boy, here I was turning into exactly the same screaming nut case my own mother was."

However, after her last angry session with her daughter, Carolyn experienced something different and surprising. "I'd had a terrible day. Everyone was barking at me at work, customers and my boss, and the tips were lousy. Duke was bothering me too. Coming on to me, which for some reason I didn't find exciting the way I sometimes did, just annoying. Then I got caught in a sudden rainstorm that soaked and ruined my waitress uniform and shoes. It was one of those days when absolutely nothing went right. Stan's mother was standing at the door waiting for me. I was barely into the house when she started her list of what I had to do for the baby, what I had to get for her, what I had to start feeding her, the whole bit. I just exploded. I told her to butt out of what wasn't her business, get the hell out of the house. As far as I was concerned she could stay away forever. She burst into tears and handed me Suzie, who promptly went into a screaming rage."

After her mother-in-law stormed out of the house, Carolyn turned to her angry, screaming daughter, "feeling like this was the last straw. I was in a blind fury. I raised my hand, ready to *wallop* Suzie . . . " But Carolyn stopped and shut her eyes hard, which didn't, however, stop her tears. "Suzie looked at me in absolute terror, put her hands up in front of her, drew back, winced, like a little animal preparing to get hit. It was involuntary. How had she learned to be so afraid of me? What had I been doing to her? How often in the past had I threatened her, or even hit her, that she'd learned to draw away from me so instinctively? It was such a horrible moment. I looked at my raised hand and, well, I lost it. I started to sob." Carolyn says she grabbed her baby, whose angry screams had turned into sobbing too, and "we just held each other, desperately crying, holding on for dear life. I just poured myself out in that embrace. It's like we were *both* so needy for contact, for love, for something to take away the fear and the rage and the pain . . . "

What Carolyn says she felt, as she and her daughter began to calm down, was the first complete moment of unconditional love she'd been able to feel for her daughter since the day of her birth. "This precious, precious child—this wonderful miracle of a child—suddenly, somehow, I made contact with how much love I knew she needed from me, how much love I needed to give, and how much love *I* needed too. It's like buried beneath all my anger was this terrible ache of sadness. And buried beneath that was some distant experience of love that I wanted so desperately to get back, bring up again, plug into. It may sound crazy, but this moment of accepting the anger and the sadness and the love was somehow beautiful. Part of the beauty was experiencing and accepting and getting through the *pain*. It's so hard to talk about. But it was a turning point for me."

In this breakthrough of experiencing and accepting all of her feelings, coming face to face with her own need for love as well as her own capacity to give love, Carolyn experienced what she calls "the first moment of full sobriety I think I've ever known. It was like this flood of compassion for me, for my daughter, for how difficult it was to muck through this life but how miraculous it was when we hung on and weathered the pain and got through to the love, which was always there to begin with! That was the feeling. It was spiritual, really. Somehow, *through* my emotions—even the most hurtful, violent, fearful, and sad feelings—I got back home to some feeling of love that underlay everything. This sounds so hokey to anyone who hasn't experienced it, I know. But it's like how I felt when I knew I was an alcoholic and an addict and needed help. It was the overwhelming feeling that I *didn't have to destroy myself*, that I didn't have to fear feelings or believe they had the power to destroy me. I'd found some experience of love that was stronger than all that, love that could rescue me and nurture me and help me to get better . . . "

Carolyn says these weren't feelings she could articulate at first. "That night, all I knew was I felt some kind of relief. I felt this incredible tenderness, somehow poignant and sad and joyful at the same time, about being a mother and what Suzie meant to me. I felt such remorse for the frightened woman I'd been, the angry wife and worker and mother. I called my mother-in-law that night and apologized. When Stan came home, I didn't jump down his throat. He knew there was a difference in me, that something had released. I wasn't so *tense* anymore. It was like I was able to tap into some source of willingness . . . "

The experience of all this had the quality of surrender, Carolyn says. "It wasn't me railing against the world, hanging on with white knuckles to the swings of my emotions, always wanting to be somewhere or with someone I wasn't. It was me letting go. That was the feeling of relief, that I *could* let go. But it wasn't like I'd found some kind of drugged-out bliss. I knew my problems were still there. I didn't magically find Stan attractive, for one thing. And I knew, somehow, that while my fantasies about Duke and Bill had calmed down for the moment, they would probably come back. This moment of acceptance was exactly that: a moment. But it registered. I felt, and at the best times still feel, a real ability to *accept* all the pieces of me, all the unfinished business and confusion and anger and sadness. All that wasn't something to judge as bad. It was part of the beauty of life. For that moment, I felt that life was worth living. The good, the bad, and the incomprehensible were something I wanted to participate in. I was open to talking about it, thinking more about it." Like Ian, Carolyn resuscitated her relationship with her sponsor. "Now that I was less afraid of myself, I was less afraid to talk about these things, especially my sexual frustrations." Also like Ian, Carolyn began to see that the two halves of herself—what she calls "the Frederick's of Hollywood me" and the "Mother Teresa me"—didn't have to be at war. "I'm made up of a lot of different selves and traits. And I have this sense, for the first time, that maybe they're all worth looking at, maybe even worth cherishing. At least I'm a little less likely to dismiss any one part of me as bad. I want to *look* at who I am in a different way. With more acceptance, less judgment."

These are all wonderful feelings, Carolyn says, "but they're fleeting, they go in and out. I'm talking about how I felt that one night and how I've been able to feel at a number of Twelve-Step meetings and in two or three conversations I've had with my sponsor. The old frustrations still crop up, and I can't always feel so accepting and philosophical about them. When Suzie screams it can still make me see red. Duke's sexy innuendoes are still a disturbing turn-on. Stan still sometimes seems like a lump. My mother-in-law still seems like an intrusion. But, I don't know. I just don't react quite so blindly or angrily to all of that anymore. It's like there's some almost *amused* self at the center of me that doesn't take it all so seriously. And, for the moment, this kind of amused lady in my heart is giving me hope. I don't know how I'll sort this stuff out, especially the sex and romance parts. But for some reason, right now, I don't think I have to *worry* about it so much . . . "

SUBTLER HALVES: HYDE DOESN'T ONLY WEAR BLACK

Ian and Carolyn have given two views of the divided self that seem to ring a bell in a lot of recovering people: it's very clear to them which half of them is "bad" and which is "good." The secret "bad" selves they've felt the impulse to hide, and have reflexively hated for so long, are clearly delineated, clearly different from the "good" public personae they feel they're "supposed" to be.

The experience of a divided Jekyll and Hyde self isn't always this black and white, however. Jackie, a forty-five-year-old woman in the suburbs of Boston who has been sober in AA for almost five years, says that she isn't aware of having judged her sexual feelings as bad. After being married for twenty-three years, she's left her husband and twenty-one-year-old son and is now living with a lover, a thirty-year-old woman named Alison, all of which goes completely against the grain of her upbringing. "It's not that I don't feel guilty, sometimes," Jackie says. "But I don't feel guilty about being lesbian. My guilt is about breaking up my family and its effect on my son. My fears also have to do with my age right now and how much age difference there is between Alison and me. My fears have to do with having to face that so much of my life has already passed by. I was barely conscious through most of it. I got married too young. I drank and smoked pot nonstop through that marriage, mostly to numb me so that I wouldn't have to face the fact that I didn't really want to be married, at least not to the person I was with. I'd been sort of distantly aware of having feelings for women my whole life, but I'd anesthetized myself for so long that I never allowed myself to imagine *doing* anything about it.

"It's only been in sobriety that I realized I had no choice: I couldn't escape the fact that I wanted out of my marriage, and I couldn't escape my feelings for women. Meeting Alison in a women's AA meeting changed my life in so many ways, beyond the obvious. I've accepted more than that I'm alcoholic and gay. I've accepted that it's all right to live your life the way you want to live it." Jackie pauses, sighs. "Well, at least in principle I have. Something's still holding me back. I'm still not sure what it is . . . "

For as long as Jackie can remember—"back to when I was about five years old"—she always felt the pressure to take care of other people. "My mother would get these terrible migraines, all through my childhood, and I grew up feeling like I had to tiptoe everywhere I went. It started with simple don'ts: Don't make any noise, mommy isn't feeling well. Be careful not to upset mommy, she might get sick again. Then, when I got older, it was expected I'd make breakfast for daddy before he left for work and get my younger sister and brother up and off to school. Mommy couldn't handle it on her own. I was the real mommy in the house. My mother was always 'indisposed.'"

Jackie only later learned that her mother was hooked to prescription tranquilizers. "I'm not surprised that I ended up going the same route. It's clear to me that I wanted to get attention the way my mother always seemed to be able to—by getting sick. But because I also grew up thinking I had to take care of everybody, I felt guilty for being sick. The answer was to blot myself out with booze and pills. Then I could collapse and people would have to take care of me."

The moment Jackie met someone who wanted to marry her she dropped out of college and became his wife. "I could only imagine one way to survive: find someone to take care of me," she says. "But my own caretaker mode was going strong too, so it was this erratic seesaw of me worrying and nagging and taking care of everything and then me blacking out on booze and pills and forcing my husband to pick me up off the floor and take care of me. I was unpredictable, to say the least." Jackie's son was born just a year into the marriage, and Jackie brought him up "in a haze of worry and fear. I loved my little boy, but I felt so hyperresponsible for everything that happened to him that I must have turned his childhood into hell. I'd force myself to watch him every night to see that he didn't suddenly die of crib death. When he was a toddler, I was so frightened every time he took any risk: taking his first steps, getting up on a tricycle. I couldn't help myself. It was like if I didn't monitor his every breath and movement, he wouldn't survive. More and more frequently, I'd sneak moments to drink or pop a Valium. I was afraid I'd go completely out of control if I didn't find some way to calm myself down." Eventually Jackie calmed herself down to near catatonia. "I overdosed on sleeping pills and a half a quart of vodka about five years ago. I don't think I was trying to kill myself; at least I don't remember consciously making that decision. But I'd been killing myself for years. I'd always wanted to check out, the way my mother did." Jackie says she was aware she'd hit bottom when she woke up in the hospital, after getting her stomach pumped. She went into drug and alcohol rehabilitation and started going to meetings, "mostly AA," she says. "For some reason I felt more at home with people who called themselves alcoholic than with those who called themselves drug addicts. Maybe because a lot of people I met in rehab who took drugs took speed. I was always trying to slow myself down, erase my mind, the way I heard a lot of alcoholics kept trying to do."

As she grew sober, the realization that she was lesbian grew stronger. "At first, all I knew was that I felt more comfortable in women's meetings than in general meetings. Then, when I heard Alison speak, I felt something much more urgent— love. Not friendship love. It was an erotic and emotional charge I don't ever remember feeling before." Jackie asked Alison out for coffee after the meeting. "I found myself pouring my heart out to her. That I felt trapped in my marriage. That I was certain I had made a huge mistake hooking myself to a man." Alison listened and suggested Jackie call her whenever she wanted to talk. Over the next months, Jackie did so. She went to more women's meetings in downtown Boston. She joined a lesbian Children of Alcoholics group. She went into therapy. By the middle of her second year of sobriety, she made the decision to leave her husband. By the same time, she and Alison decided to become lovers.

THE FEAR OF PLEASURE

"The transition hasn't been an upheaval in the way I thought it would be," Jackie says. "Frankly, my husband and I were moving toward separating anyway. He took my decision pretty calmly. And my son had gotten so used to his weird mother all through his life that he didn't seem very upset either. He's a smart kid—in college, has a lot of liberal friends. I even think he might be proud of me. Sure, what I said before is still true. I'm afraid what the long-term effects of all this might be on him. I'm afraid of the resentments he's hiding. He's the child of an alcoholic after all! But when I look at the reality of how he's taking it now, there doesn't seem to be much need to worry. Alison keeps reminding me he's got a Higher Power too. I don't have to keep second-guessing him or trying to control his feelings about me." The problem Jackie is facing is something she is aware has much more to do with herself than with others' opinions of her.

"I don't understand it," she says. "Within a couple of months of moving in with Alison, I just shut down sexually. Here I have what I thought I always wanted—a loving relationship with an exciting woman who is smart and supportive and understands me like nobody I've ever known before—and something in me has just plain shut down! Alison has been pushing for us to go to a couples counselor, even a sex therapist. I'm so embarrassed by this. It's so hard for me to talk about. I get so *angry* at myself. What do I want? Don't I have exactly what I want now? What's my damned problem?"

Jackie is on the verge of tears. "Hell," she says. "It's not like I don't know *anything* about myself, about why I distance myself from Alison the way I do. Sometimes I'll look at her, and she'll seem so young, so athletic, so beautiful, and then I'll look down at myself, down *on* myself really, and I'll seem like this soft, big-breasted, overweight, aging matron. Somebody's mother. That's what I am: somebody's mother! Not somebody's *lover*. I don't know anything about being young and in love. I don't know anything about intimacy! I just feel so inadequate. How do you do this stuff sober? When I drank and drugged and had sex with my husband, which wasn't much in the last decade or two of our marriage, it didn't matter much what he did to me, what happened. It was the old 'lie back and think of England' trip. But now, now I want to participate, now I want to accept Alison's attentions. And she keeps trying. She really does seem to find me attractive! I keep thinking there's something wrong with *her*. Like she's got a mother fetish. I have worse thoughts. Alison is black, and sometimes I wonder if she isn't interested in me totally because I'm *white*. Maybe that's some kind of fetish too! I can't begin to accept that she might want me, love me, just for being who I am. There has to be something wrong with her to want to be with me . . . "

Jackie is aware of something else. "Ever since I stopped drinking, I just haven't seemed to be able to let myself enjoy anything. Not completely. I know it's common for recovering alcoholics to have a problem with, say, dancing after they get sober. Go to a disco without being drunk or high? How do you do that? Well, that's the feeling. I can't dance. I can't seem to let myself do anything just for fun. It's like I'm afraid of pleasure. It's more than just comparing myself to Alison and finding myself lacking. There's something missing at the very core of me, something that was never there to begin with. The capacity for *joy*."

The caretaker mode Jackie felt bound to was, she realized, still compelling to her. "I grew up thinking I could never do something just for me. Letting loose, having a good time, making noise, playing—all of that would have made my mother literally, physically sick! That's the message I grew up with. The only way I could earn any kind of approval, anything approaching love, was to sacrifice my wants to her wants. I had to take care of her to feel good about myself, to gain even a crumb of love or attention from her. Pleasure for its own sake was unthinkable. Drinking and drugging were an antidote to all this, but they didn't give me pleasure, really. They just blocked out all feeling. Now that I'm sober, I don't have a way to escape like that anymore. And I keep banging up against my own inability to let loose, even to accept a *little* affection and love from Alison."

Jackie had a painful breakthrough about this recently. "We went through a bad shock about a month ago. Alison's brother was killed in a car crash. She hadn't talked much about her family. She'd sort of summed them up as a bunch of drunken jerks. But when news reached her of her brother's death, she just totally collapsed." Jackie says she didn't know what to do. "Holding Alison, trying to comfort her, trying to get her to eat, I went through the whole arsenal of nurturing stuff I'd depended on since childhood with my own mother and then my own family to 'make things better.' But nothing worked. Alison really loved this brother. She said it was 'him and me against the world' when they were growing up. He protected her from their abusive father. He took the blame for things she'd done wrong so that she wouldn't get hit. He was the only member of her family who cared about her. I didn't know what to do. I'd never seen her get into such a bad depression. And the worst part of it was, she began to withdraw really severely from me. Sometimes when I'd reach out to touch her, to comfort her, she'd back away, like a scared animal. It was like she hated me all of a sudden, hated my trying to intrude! It was so frightening to me. Finally, one night she actually shouted, 'Leave me alone! You can't help me. You don't even love me!'"

Jackie was dumbstruck. "Not love her? What shocked and hurt me wasn't that she could think that about me. What shocked me was, looking at her cowering in a far corner of the bed, clutching onto the covers, looking at me in such terror and aloneness, I had a terrible and clear picture of *myself*. She was me. A totally abandoned, loveless little girl. That look of abject terror, of complete aloneness—it was the picture of how I felt about myself. I sat down at the foot of the bed and totally lost it. I just sat there sobbing."

Jackie came to a crucial, compassionate acceptance of this "loveless little girl" inside of her, a fearful being she could also accept was part of her lover. "I'd turned Alison into this paragon of strength, someone totally together—sexually, politically, emotionally, you name it. But she was just as full of pain and doubt and fear as I was. I *saw* her, it seemed like, for the first time." The two women's tears were cathartic. "We started to talk to each other, really talk to each other, that night. She talked about how alone she felt, how much she held herself back because she could see I was in so much pain. I talked about how jealous I was of her. I realized I'd been so self-absorbed, I'd never really let all of who Alison was in."

They made love that night. Jackie says that, for the first time, "I'd lost my inhibitions. Somehow I was able to surrender to the sheer pleasure of it." She lowers her eyes and laughs softly. "Honesty turns out to be an incredible aphrodisiac. Our outbursts had opened something in us. We *trusted* each other. I didn't feel like I was trying to hide my body or self or emotions or anything. I was *there* in a way I'd never allowed myself to be with anyone. And Alison knew it and encouraged me. It was wonderful. But what was also wonderful was that, for that moment, I really let up on myself. Now, looking back on it, I see that it was like I introduced two halves of me—the concerned caretaker and the frightened little girl who wanted so desperately to play but was told she couldn't—I let them come together. I felt *whole*. And feeling whole made me feel like I could give and receive love freely."

Jackie is aware, she says, "that I've just opened the door on all this. My old reflexes haven't magically gone away. I still shut down sometimes. But now I know I can get through. And the way through seems to be to admit to myself and to Alison what I'm feeling. I'm learning that she won't reject me if I tell her. And Alison is learning the same thing. There's hope for me, for both of us. And the old self-hate is slowly lifting, like the sun burning off a thick fog."

Jackie also says that what she's learning in "program" has a completely new meaning to her. "It seems there's no end to the levels you can 'surrender' on—that old layers-of-the-onion thing. There are greater and greater depths of freedom and trust we can reach if we just keep pursuing sobriety. Thank God Alison is in recovery too. We've got a lot of support. We're not alone anymore. That's the bottom line: we're not alone."

The divided self is an illusion. Our "bad" parts are as much a part of us as our "good" parts. They deserve equal love, acceptance, and consideration. That's what Ian, Carolyn, Jackie, and Alison have discovered, and that's their lesson to the rest of us. "Hyde"—your unacceptable self—doesn't go away just because you've labeled it that. He resists erasing. He plants himself stubbornly, defying you to ignore him. Alcohol and drugs can work either to push him away or allow you, secretly, to play with him, which is why a good many of us clung to alcohol and drugs. That blessed state of "not caring"—"Who gives a damn?"—is one to which so many of us aspired. We searched desperately for ways to tolerate who we were, even if it meant battering ourselves into a state of senselessness. That was as close to "acceptance" as many of us could get.

In sobriety we don't have that option. The "dark" parts of us remain like a range of great, craggy alps: we can't blast them away or pretend they're not there. Sooner or later we find that we have no choice but to climb them. However, when we finally begin to do this, we usually discover something remarkable. With the benevolent guidance of other people who've faced and climbed their own mountains, and in the context of the Twelve Steps, exploring these dark peaks turns out to be an amazing, healing, and fascinating adventure. There are hidden gardens here, astonishing in their beauty and variety. We discover we've been running away from some of the most interesting and valuable information we could discover about ourselves.

As Carolyn suggests, we always face new levels of fear and resistance as we continue this journey into ourselves. Simply starting on the journey isn't enough to banish fear: new fears continually crop up. But it's the experience of many recovering people that, as we face and deal with these deeper levels of fear, we discover nothing "horrible" or "unspeakable." We simply discover more and more of what makes us up. And the completely unexpected dividend is that we can end up loving what we find.

Let's travel deeper into the mountains right now. Let's look at what most of us label our greatest secrets of all: our sexual fantasies.

CHAPTER 4

Secret Gardens: Our Sexual Fantasies

Many of us have decided that what we're doing and feeling sexually isn't what we ought to be doing and feeling. It's very common for us to divide feelings into "nice" (love and friendship) and "not nice" (sex and lust), berating ourselves mercilessly for the parts of ourselves we've judged "not nice." Sometimes the division isn't quite so obvious (even if it's just as guilt inducing): we may simply feel divided between our "good," responsible, caretaking selves and our "bad," self-indulgent, pleasure-seeking selves. Whether we're single or involved with a lover or spouse doesn't have any automatic effect, good or bad, on dealing with this split; the effects of feeling divided can be devastating and even threaten our sobriety, whatever our relationship status.

We've gotten some good evidence that facing this split head on—talking about it, bringing it into the light—is the best way to begin to heal it. But we have to do a thorough job of it. Our continuing serenity depends on going as deep as we can into even the most taboo areas of our selves and psyches.

Going deeper into our negative assumptions about sex, intimacy, and love inevitably leads us to a face-to-face confrontation with our sexual fantasies. Freud defined fantasy generally as "a correction of unsatisfying reality." It is our unconscious response to a reality we want to change, our attempt to make things better. However, because of the repression bred into us by family and society, inhibitions that dictate sexual should's and shouldn'ts, many of our sexual fantasies' "corrections" cause us shame. We grow to fear the suggestions our sexual fantasies make to us because they urge us, with a ferocious power, to be "bad." Sexual fantasies therefore can seem toxic: all sorts of frightening scenarios and shameful demons may inhabit this realm, various imaginary situations or fixations that you've probably long since labeled abnormal and kept secret.

From my conversations with scores of recovering men and women, it's heartbreakingly clear to me that we tend to react to our sexual fantasies with a fierce self-hate. But it's equally clear that our fantasies, however negatively we may judge them, are marvels of psychological imagination and ingenuity. The people you'll meet in this chapter have found that their sexual fantasies offer tantalizing clues about their inner lives. They've even come to see their fantasies as heroic attempts to accommodate strong and sometimes very frightening feelings and fears.

Unfortunately, this helpful aspect is quickly undercut by how disturbing the content of fantasies can be, how much self-loathing they can induce, how much physical or psychological abuse they can be based on and perpetuate. Even when the nature of a sexual fantasy is more gentle—what you might think of as more normal or acceptable—facing it can be just as difficult, scary, embarrassing. So many recovering alcoholics and addicts mentally whip themselves for whatever their fantasies may be, believing they're too outrageous, too humiliating, or too foolish to admit. As a result, we either shut the door on them, attempting to white-knuckle them into submission, or let them sneak in when nobody's looking, furtively (and usually shamefully) acting them out. This struggle doesn't stop when we get sober. For some of us, it can even increase after we've stopped drinking and drugging. The bottom line is, too often, that we hate ourselves for our fantasies. We're miserably stuck as a result.

The tragedy of refusing to explore our sexual and romantic fantasies isn't only that pushing them down or away tends to erode our serenity and hence our sobriety. It's also that we're depriving ourselves of some enormously rich opportunities for self-examination and growth. Sexual fantasies have so much to tell us: they are full of data about how we've learned to handle our deepest feelings, about the source of the assumptions we bring to love and sex, and how we view ourselves— who we think we are. We can cultivate self-compassion and self-acceptance by facing these mine-laden fields. Our well-being and sobriety depend on exploring this territory as completely as we can. We can't seem to afford to be dishonest with ourselves about anything. (Not that this exploration needs to or can be done quickly. All of us, and especially newcomers to sobriety, need to be reminded that we're doing just fine by staying sober one day at a time. First things first: we've got a lifetime to recover.)

Looking closely at your fantasies and what they're telling you about your needs, fears, and wants can have some very surprising rewards, not the least of which is a new clarity about just what it is you're really *after* in your private sexual imaginings. Once you've taken this look, you may conclude, for example, that you can no longer so neatly compartmentalize lust away from love. Or, conversely, you may discover how you may have been equating sex with love and begin to be able to see the differences between them more objectively. It's likely that a lot more is going on here than you realize.

Let's look at three main, general issues that exploring our sexual fantasies always seems to bring us to: *power*, *anger*, and the problem we just identified of *confusing sex with love*.

POWER

Until three years ago when she was thirty-one and got sober, Grace was a closet drinker: she only drank alone, at home, and at night. She had what she says was "a completely divided life. I had the job I still have, as a receptionist at an advertising agency, and I know I come across as sort of Marian the Librarian. I've always been shy in public, your typical wallflower." In private, however, Grace has had a very active fantasy life, one she says "would shock anyone who knows me at work." In her drinking days she says that each week she'd "stop by a newsstand far from where I live and stock up on singles magazines and papers, some of them downright pornographic, others like *New York Magazine* or the *Village Voice*, anything that had personal ads. I'd go home, pour myself some sherry, and meticulously go through each one searching for a particular type of man." Grace searched for older "daddy" types: an "in-charge" man who wanted a little "kitten" to dominate.

"That's how I thought of myself: a kitten. Coy and sweet, little and flirtatious. I saw myself as a sexy, ultrafeminine little gamine in these fantasies. A Lolita, I guess. I have small breasts, and I'm short and slim. I look like a little girl. I can fit into junior sizes, and at one point I had a whole wardrobe of girlish nighties I'd put on when I drank and got into the personal ads. I'd settle on the three or four most likely male candidates, fantasize about them as I emptied the sherry bottle, and then type out detailed letters about what I wanted them to do to me. I had a private post box to receive their replies. My whole life was centered on waiting for one or another of them to write back."

Grace almost never went through with meeting the men who wrote to her. "I must have gotten over two hundred letters over the past couple years," she says. "Out of all of those, I only went through with meeting four men. I called more than that, especially when I got drunk. I'd put on this Marilyn Monroe voice, sweet and high and slurred, and I'd try to make them crazy with wanting me. It turned into phone sex more than once, at least for the men at the other end of the line. It was exciting. Unbelievably exciting. I felt such . . . *power*. It's like I could taunt and taunt them and keep them completely at my beck and call. They'd get *riveted* to me. I felt like I could make them do anything I wanted."

On the phone, that is. "The four men I met were all disasters. For one thing, none of them was what they'd promised physically. I was after big, burly teddy bears of men. Like I said, real daddy types. I don't know who these guys thought they were in their heads, but they all turned out to be shy, retiring, small, skinny! It was terrible. It was incredibly embarrassing, somehow, to see an actual human being trying to be a fantasy was such a crushing disappointment. And not only for me. It hit me in the stomach to see the light go out of their eyes when they first saw me. I could tell I wasn't what they were looking for either. It was so humiliating, all around. I met each of these guys in a bar, and after a quick drink, we ended up stammering 'sorry' and 'good-bye.' I sped home to get drunk. I felt so . . . *sick*, I guess. It was those moments, after actually attempting to meet someone to live out my fantasy with, that were the worst. That's when I felt like I was really seeing what a neurotic mess I was."

It was after the last of these meetings that Grace decided to get help from a therapist. "I didn't go into detail right off about my fantasies, I just talked about being depressed. When my therapist began to clue in to how much I drank, she ended up giving me an ultimatum: stop drinking and go to AA, or I couldn't continue to see her. Something in me was ready to hear that, I suppose, because that's exactly what I did. Maybe it was the little girl in me again, looking for someone to tell me what to do. I don't know. All I know is that it took."

That was nearly three years ago. But sobriety has been a decidedly mixed bag for Grace. "I feel so much better physically, but stopping drinking didn't do a thing to stop my sexual fantasies. At first, because I'd associated reading those personals and writing letters so strongly with drinking, I didn't resume getting into the ads. It was like I'd forgotten how! But then, about six months into sobriety, I was sitting in my dentist's waiting room, and I picked up a *New York Magazine*. By reflex, I went straight to the personals. The first ad I read nearly floored me. 'Big, strong, caring man seeks sweet little kitten. Looking for Daddy? Here he is.' I swear it; he actually said the two trigger words, *kitten* and *daddy*. I had no choice. I was off and fantasizing again . . . "

Grace said she had her strongest drink signals in sobriety when she went home, that night, to write a letter to the man in the ad: "God, I wanted to drink! I turned down the lights, like I used to do, put on the romantic music I used to listen to, and started a letter to this man. Between each sentence I'd stop and my right hand would grab out to the side of the desk, searching for my sherry glass! It was frightening. It was totally involuntary. But somehow my resolve not to drink stayed with me. What began to happen is that the urgent desire for a drink got channeled back into the letter. I wrote the most pornographic come-on of a letter I'd ever written. Sobriety, suddenly, seemed to be able to *help* me write it! It's like, I was mentally clear enough to really put everything in my imagination into words. I wasn't blurred at all. What new torture was this? I'd gotten sober so that I could be a more efficient fantasizer? That's what it seemed like! I mean, I was enjoying it, but enjoying it like gulping down booze. It was totally compulsive. I remembered what I'd heard so much in AA meetings: a horse thief who stops drinking is a sober horse thief. My fantasies hadn't gone away; I hadn't turned into some nice, respectable, totally together woman simply because I'd stopped drinking. In fact, if anything, they just seemed to have a tighter hold on me!"

Grace had had enough therapy to have a good idea why she had the fantasies she did. "My father was a drunk, and I was terrified of him. He was so unpredictable. Whenever he came home, I'd hide. Or when I couldn't avoid him, like at dinner, I'd sit at the table in a state of panic. I didn't dare open my mouth. Sometimes he'd suddenly get all sweet, like I was a little doll, and . . . well, of course he called me 'kitten'! But most of the time he was in a rage. I rarely had a conversation with him beyond answering yes or no to the few questions he'd spit at me. Then, once, when I was about twelve and sick with a bad flu and could barely get out of bed, he stormed into my room drunk, and started calling me a whore . . . and worse. It was a nightmare. I felt so powerless.

He was so big; he threatened to hit me . . . " Grace shudders with the memory. "It's not easy to go back through all this. I'd really blocked most of it out until recently. But now, in sobriety, with my fantasies roaring up so strongly again, it seems to have tugged out all these vivid memories of my father too."

Our task here isn't to assess Grace psychologically. These are all issues she's begun to work on with her therapist. Issues of child abuse (and incest) have attracted a lot of needed attention, and "adult children" who've suffered from abuse are well advised to seek professional therapeutic help in addition to the support they can get from Twelve-Step programs. The point here is simply that Grace knew she was very vulnerable. "It was like the more sober I've become, the more urgently my memories are coming back and the more urgently I feel the reflex to block them out. I could always depend on alcohol to erase all this before. I guess, at least this is what my therapist suggests, my urge to fantasize is the same self-protective thing. Lose myself in a fantasy to get away from or deal with my real feelings. But understanding that intellectually doesn't help me much. I can't tell you how strong the grip is, when I imagine myself with this perfect daddy figure. As much as I'm beginning to understand it all psychologically, that this is a way to get back some of the power I completely lacked as a girl, what good is that? I'm still obsessed."

As Grace has allowed herself to face more specifics about her childhood fears, however, she's gradually found the courage to talk about these fears at least in general terms in AA meetings and to her sponsor. "To tell you the truth, talking to other sober people is the only place where I've felt even a glimmer of hope. Because what I get from AA is spiritual. It doesn't depend on figuring out anything. It depends on clarity and the kind of analysis you do in a fourth Step, but not on overanalyzing or nit-picking for the sake of nit-picking. What AA helps me to do is surrender. Let go of all this, not block it out with booze or fantasy, just face it, and then offer it up. When I can begin to feel this surrender, I start to feel less stress and, at least for that moment, less obsession. But something else is happening too. My therapist has been encouraging me to look at how ingenious my sexual fantasy is, what a perfect adaptation it was for me, given my terror of my father as a little girl. How resourceful of my imagination to have me turn into a sexy little minx and disarm the big bad wolf! Appreciating this allows me to let up on myself. Maybe I can have some compassion for why I've got the fantasy I do. This does ease some of the tension. Anything that invites me to hate myself less will help me. But the force of the fantasy! I mean, it's one thing to get a glimmer of comfort from my therapist or sponsor or in AA in a group of people. It's another to be alone in my apartment, once again, getting toward midnight, feeling alone and scared and needy. Boy, that's like giving the sexual part of me fertilizer! It gets so powerful and confusing. I know the answer to this is spiritual: to turn it over, to reach out for help, to make an effort not to withdraw and shut down. But, Lord, it's hard!"

Grace's growing ability to feel compassion for the roots of her fantasy, that it grew as a self-protective adaptation, a way to defuse terrifying fears, gives us a crucial key. So many of us expend enormous energy hating ourselves for the content of our sexual fantasies. As Grace's example shows, that energy is far more productively spent when we channel it into self-acceptance. We need to feel compassion for the ways our psyches have evolved, and maybe even a good dose of awe for how imaginative and custom tailored the solutions are that our psyches have come up with in the attempt to help us. The problem isn't that a fantasy is "bad" or "wrong." The problem comes when we feel that we haven't any choice but to cling to it, when we believe it's our only recourse, our only salvation. A fantasy, when you hate it, becomes remarkably tenacious: it grows more powerful in a climate of hate and fear, convincing you more and more that it's your only hope of release, peace, or satisfaction while, at the same time, making you berate yourself for having to depend on it. No wonder it "turns you on" *and*, often simultaneously, makes you miserable.

"*Choice* is the key word," Grace says. "Reminding myself I've got choices. It's like my biggest revelation when I stopped drinking, when I found I *wanted* to stop drinking. I was choosing not to drink. I felt such enormous freedom in that moment. It was like, You mean I don't *have* to hit myself over the head with a sledgehammer to survive? Getting to that same feeling of choice about my fantasies, about how I might want to express myself, feel about myself sexually, seems to be a more complicated and gradual thing. But the principle is the same. And I feel more choice as I pour more energy into my sobriety, into increasing a feeling of serenity, self-acceptance. That serenity and self-acceptance come from feeling as much compassion as I can about how hard it is to deal with my fantasies. It means meeting even my most secret fantasy with love, not fear. Love drains away the virulence, the obsession. I don't have to be afraid so much anymore."

This doesn't mean that Grace's fantasies have gone away, or even that they should! What she is letting into her life is a feeling of greater *space*, a wider climate of acceptance in which her fantasies are allowed to exist, be what they are, but not crowd out any other possibility of dealing with her feelings. As Grace eases up on herself, she's discovering quite spontaneously that she's more interested in seeking alternatives to her old habitual reactions: "What else can I do? Is there another way I might respond to this fear?" Just asking these questions, talking about possible alternatives, acknowledging her feelings as well as her fantasies with her sponsor and close friends in AA has allowed Grace to come up with some alternatives. Sometimes they're as simple as picking up the phone or going to a meeting. Sometimes they involve trying out dates with men who depart from her usual type. But the gradual effect on Grace is that the old urgency of her fantasies is lifting. The world, including her inner imaginative world of fantasy, is beginning to seem wider, more habitable, less threatening.

EROTICIZING RAGE: ANGER AND SEX

Martin, a forty-year-old therapist and recovering drug addict and alcoholic, can take us a little further in this journey to "alternatives." The feeling he's dealing with, however, is closer to anger than fear. "Actually," Martin says, "the word for it is *rage* . . . I used to think my sadomasochistic fantasies were something only I had. Then I thought they were something only gay men had. Now I'm learning that all kinds of people, in recovery and out, men and women, straight and gay, get into all this as well. There's a hell of a lot of anger out there!" Martin is a social worker who works in a New York therapeutic clinic and has a small private practice as well. "Before I got into this profession, I'd long suspected that shrinks were all loonier than the clients who came to them. Now that I'm a shrink, I'm living proof," Martin laughs. But his smile fades. "It's really not so funny. I know from going to Twelve-Step meetings and listening to other recovering people that it's common to feel your public and private selves are at complete odds and that we'll go to any lengths to keep anyone from finding out about the private part. We bottle up so much and battle so much shame. But I don't know, sometimes, where I get the chutzpah to put myself in a position of advising other people when so much in my own life is so screwed up. I feel like a big impostor. What the hell do I know? If my clients could see me at the after hours club I still go to . . ."

Martin has been, until recently, especially full of shame about his sexual fantasies. "You'd think what I hear in my work would make me feel a little less 'abnormal.' I mean, naturally I hear a lot about sex from my clients, especially when they see me for a long enough time to trust me and let down their defenses. And, boy, am I ever in awe of the human imagination. I've seen men and women eroticize *everything*. One guy I worked with was turned on by his sexual partners sneezing. Another said he barked like a puppy dog every time he came to orgasm. Stuff that causes people so much shame: the black gay man who yearned to be cuffed and abused by a white 'master,' Jews who fantasized about Nazis, women who imagined being gang raped. This is very upsetting territory. One feminist who campaigned in the streets against pornography because of how demeaning it is to women couldn't, herself, keep from fantasizing about being Scarlett O'Hara ravaged by Rhett Butler. She hated herself for her fantasies; she was in agony about how 'politically incorrect' she couldn't seem to help being deep down. Even the tamer fantasies—one woman I worked with could only allow her husband to touch her when he was wearing her fluffy bathroom slippers—cause so much distress to people determined to fight them. And talk about fetishes! Shoes, boots, every imaginable kind of underwear, leather, rubber, satin . . .

"Sometimes, like recently, when I'm not beating myself up out of reflex, I'm helped by the reminder that *nothing* is taboo to the human sexual imagination: whatever we psychically need to eroticize, we'll eroticize. Doesn't matter what our mothers think. Sexual expression always has its own rules, at least in the imagination. Which is, anyway, where it really occurs. Sex happens in the *head*."

Martin has known all this for years. He completed an M.S.W. program at a major university, continually takes courses in psychoanalysis, reads a good deal of psychological literature, and can quote any number of eminent theoreticians on sex. "I knew all this, that sex was a subject for exploration, not condemnation, even when I drank and drugged," Martin says. "But that knowledge stayed completely in the head. Until very recently, I couldn't permit myself to get any personal help. God, I was eloquent enough with my clients about how they needed to let up on themselves, give themselves permission to have their fantasies, realize that having a feeling won't kill you. But, damned if I could believe it myself."

Martin says he has to "sidle up" to admitting what his fantasies are. "Let me tell you about my background. That'll help get me into it. It wasn't exactly *Ordinary People*, because we are Jewish, but if you can imagine Jewish WASPs, well, that's what my parents aspired to. Dad is a successful lawyer, mom a perfect housewife and PTA-goer. Very controlled. Determined to get everything right. The right suburb outside of Cleveland. They've spent their lives trying to be some kind of antiseptic American Dream, at least that's how it seems to me. My younger brother just cracked. He couldn't take the pressure to be perfect. He's still active, whacking himself out on any drug he can find, a real garbage head. We don't talk about him anymore; he's 'somewhere out in California finding himself.' I worry about him, but I know enough about my own addiction to know I don't have any control over him. What bothers me is he doesn't know there's a way out. And he doesn't know that somebody in his own family understands a lot about his pain. He's totally cut us off, including me."

Martin was the "good boy." "My parents still don't know I'm gay. I'm thirty-five, and they still tell themselves I'm so involved in my career that I haven't had the time to look for the right woman. They also don't know that I was as much of a mess on booze and drugs as my brother is now. I was good at hiding all that. I got through college and grad school with good grades, even an award or two, and nobody knew. Of course, my academic adviser *would* ask 'Are you all right?' a lot. Once I overheard him talking to one of my other professors about me. God, that made me queasy: 'Why is Martin so tortured all the time?' I was amazed. I thought I was this picture of equanimity. So polite, sweet, unruffled. Never argued with anybody. Why would anyone think I was tortured?" Martin shakes his head. "I've got a snapshot of myself from those days. The tension was so great in my eyes, in my face, that I almost can't bear to look at it now. I had no idea I was revealing so much of my pain . . . "

Martin identifies with the Jekyll/Hyde model. "That whole serene public persona I kept trying to use to fool my parents and people at school hid a monster. That's how I thought of it, how I sometimes still think of it." He pauses for a moment, evidently considering whether or not to reveal something. "I'm turned on by getting tied up and beaten." Martin lets out a long low whoosh of air. "There. I said it. When I drank and was in grad school, I found this whole S&M gay network, first by going home with some sleaze bag at a leather bar who 'knew some people,' then through personal ads in sex magazines. Anyone I could find who was big and rough and played the sadist role, I'd go for. Met quite a variety of people, let me tell you. It's funny—I've found this out through being a therapist too—these tough guys were sweet, well-spoken, well-educated, totally under control in their public lives. You'd never think they got into the sexual scenes they did. But then, nobody would ever have expected it of me either."

Martin became quite a connoisseur of sadists: "I got so I had a number of guys who were expert at inflicting pain without leaving marks I'd have to explain at school the next day. It was an incredible turn-on, actually, aching from the slaps, kicks, punches, or other forms of torture I'd received the night before, like some great secret my body had while I sat in class looking like a perfectly normal and well-behaved grad student. I got off on the taboo aspects of it." Martin sighs again. "I still do."

"You want me to give you chapter and verse about why I've got the fantasies I do? You can already anticipate it, can't you? Little kid is brought up to think he can't be himself. That the only way to gain his parents' love and attention is to bury any suggestion of anger. He can't tolerate his murderous resentments against his parents, and so he turns them against himself. He looks for sinister authority figures to act like the angry parent, to give him what he deserves. I could go on. But you get the picture. Of course, none of this really *helps*. You can analyze things up the wazoo—and I have, almost literally—but you're still stuck with the primal dilemma, the feelings of rage you can't seem to do anything with but push down. I mean, I'm a therapist. I supposedly *believe* in the talking cure, that the best way to deal with all this stuff is to drag it out in the open, drain it of its venom, see that you won't die if you tell the truth about your feelings. But until recently, something in me just wasn't

buying all that. Not deep down. Deep down I was still too attached to this view of myself as a loathsome little worm who
deserved to be crushed. And what kept me wed to that vision
is that, in sexual terms, it turned me on. That's the glue: when
you eroticize something, you *want* it. You keep wanting to go
back to it. Why would you ever want to stop doing something
you *love* doing? Because in some abstract way you know it's not
good for you? That never worked with booze and drugs. I knew
I was an addict and alcoholic long before I put down booze
and drugs. I didn't care that they were messing me up, at least
not for a long time. I loved getting high. Why would I want to
stop doing something I loved?"

Martin is fairly active in AA and NA. "I chair one meeting,
make coffee at another. I have a lot of program friends. None
of them know about my sex life, but I'm pretty open with
them otherwise. I mean, I'm a good therapist; I can empathize
pretty freely. People like me, at least the me they can see. And
Twelve-Step stuff does help. I do get the message, at least
dimly, that the kind of analysis called for in the fourth Step
isn't self-critical nit-picking, it's an attempt to get clear about
who you are. Again, like I said, I'm smart about the surface of
all this stuff. I could be a great spokesperson for sobriety. But I
can't completely surrender in the sexual realm. Actually, I
don't *want* to. I don't want to surrender my sexual fantasies.
Nothing else turns me on, gives me a greater rush, makes me
feel more alive. How could I possibly give them up?"

Martin stopped drinking and drugging because it made him
so physically and spiritually sick. "I know there's a message
there. You won't really change unless you're convinced you
can get more out of the new behavior than you could out of
the old. Drugs and alcohol had battered me down so low, they
made keeping up my public appearance so hard, that I just

couldn't tolerate them anymore. I was completely battered, empty, squeezed out. I couldn't take any more."

This doesn't apply to his sexual fantasies. "When I first got sober, I soon found that I still was horny over the same stuff that turned me on when I drank and drugged. This surprised me, because sex had always been so attached to drugs and alcohol that I think I expected my sex drive to just go away once I stopped getting high. Anyway, I did get pretty compulsive about it. Spent a lot of money on phone sex at first. Obsessed over getting back together with 'top men' who wouldn't mind having a scene without getting wasted on beer or poppers. I even went to some Sexual Compulsives Anonymous meetings. And, actually, they helped. Because their whole idea was that you defined 'sexual sobriety' for yourself. There were no rules about it that applied across the board to everybody. But, I don't know, while it got me thinking in some new and profitable ways about all this stuff, I resisted it. I saw too many people turn against themselves, label themselves 'sex addicts' too readily, it seemed to me. It's like they were afraid of sex, not trying to make sex a healthy part of their lives. Whatever that could mean! Okay, I know that was just my take on it, and I'm sure I was projecting my own fears. But it didn't work for me. AA and NA worked, but not this other Twelve-Step stuff."

However, something *has* recently constituted what Martin calls "a breakthrough. Strangely, it came from dealing with a woman client of mine who's just started to see me privately. I say strangely, because I didn't expect to feel such a visceral connection to this woman when I first met her. She's a recovering alcoholic, that much I understood. Although because she's an ex-nun—she went to incredible lengths to hide her drinking in the convent—her experience of getting high departed considerably in its particulars from my nights in after-hour S&M clubs, some guy in a black leather mask chaining me up and paddling my bare ass." Martin shakes his head wearily. "But here she was—Catholic, female, straight, with years spent in a convent. Talk about repressed. I mean, the poor woman had married *Christ*, for Christ's sake. Not a lot of sex talk and foreplay in that marriage." Martin smiles guiltily.

"I'm being outrageous. The urge to say something rude about people like this is hard for me to resist. And this woman was everything you'd expect a nun to be—right out of central casting, *The Bells of St. Mary's*—Irish, pretty, sweet, docile, innocent. In fact, that's what got to me. It took her five months of seeing me once a week before she could admit that she wanted to meet a man and didn't know how to go about it. She was so unbelievably shy. My heart went out to her. But something about the struggle she was having with her own seemingly tame romantic fantasies really got to me. It amounted to a real breakthrough. She said she just wanted to meet a man to dance with. She hadn't been to a dance since she was in junior high school. By high school she'd already decided to become a nun and no longer had anything to do with boys. But she remembered a junior high dance when a tall, handsome, redheaded, older boy ('He was in ninth grade and I was in seventh,' she said, 'Just that was enough to take my breath away!') asked her to dance. To this day she remembers how his hand felt on her waist, how exhilarating it was to swing in time to the music. I know it sounds corny, like something out of *The Sound of Music*. But she looked so entranced when she talked about it. 'I felt his fingers on my back!' she said, nervous, excited, like the girl she was then. What got to me, though, was this terrible reflex of guilt that always followed her talking about even this little innocent episode."

Martin said that after talking about even the idea of going out with a man and dancing, she would get angry with herself, "sometimes to the point of banging her fists on the couch. She'd call herself foolish and silly and who would want to go out with her anyway. She had no idea what to do on a date with a man; she felt like a freak. Who could want an ex-nun? She'd scare off any man, probably. She felt the whole world would laugh at her if she ever let anyone know that she wanted to date somebody. She said she didn't fit in anywhere, and why couldn't she just forget all this nonsense? But that junior high dance kept coming back. It haunted her. She was obsessed by it. It had gotten to the point where she was nervous every time she saw a tall, red-haired man; her palms would start to sweat. All of this made her feel not only foolish, but neurotic. She couldn't get control of her feelings. And she couldn't block them out the way she used to, sneaking wine late at night in the convent, all the other sisters asleep. She'd always known, deep down, that she wasn't like them, even when she was a novitiate. She couldn't be as pious and good as they all were; she didn't have their faith. And she hadn't a clue about how to live in the world. All she had for sustenance was this stupid fantasy of dancing with a red-haired man in a junior high gym. She couldn't help thinking of herself as a pathetic wreck. Sometimes it got so bad she wanted to kill herself. And nothing really helped. AA only helped her while she was actually in a meeting, it seemed. Even praying to God wasn't much solace, although she felt like the worst heretic for admitting it . . . "

Martin pauses. "I can't explain, really, why this got to me. I mean, it was something past feeling bad for her and being touched by her innocence and her exaggerated fears. I guess that as different as my violent sexual scenarios were from her rose-tinted junior high memories, I saw that we both were raking ourselves over the coals. There wasn't one moment of patience or acceptance in either of us. The only emotion we could feel about our own needs, desires, wants was contempt. How could we be so neurotic as to *want* something that bad? That's really what we were doing to ourselves, each of us in different ways. I suddenly saw, or rather felt, for the first time that there was nothing intrinsically 'wrong' about her dancing fantasy or my sadomasochistic one. They were symbols of our hunger for contact, and they fit us to a T. They grew out of who we were, what we needed from the world. They were something to be looked at with love and wonder and curiosity—with *care*. We kept trying to cut these parts of ourselves out, like some loathsome disfigurement. I now saw how wrong we were for fighting ourselves this way! And as I felt this loving urge toward this woman, this complete and sudden knowledge that what she needed to give herself was love, not contempt, somehow it trickled down to me too. I needed love, not contempt."

The meaning of the Twelve-Step slogan "You're only as sick as your secrets" isn't that the content of anyone's secret is "sick," but that its very secretness is the problem. In the same way, Martin realized that his sadomasochistic fantasies weren't necessarily or intrinsically "bad." What made them "bad" was his reaction to them: his fear and hatred of them, his belief that they branded him a "bad" person, his conviction that they had to be buried, hidden, something to be resorted to guiltily, furtively. When he began to feel some compassion for himself instead of contempt, some appreciation for how efficiently his fantasies enabled him to deal with his anger, how his psyche had ingeniously invented them as adaptations to deal with some primal and terrifying feelings, he began to let up on himself.

"I needed this ex-nun to jolt me into a more gut-level awareness of all this. I so genuinely wanted her not to hate herself for wanting love and sex. It was so genuine that I began to realize it was okay to allow myself to want those things." One of the unanticipated dividends of all this is that Martin has given himself permission to admit that he *enjoys* his sexual fantasies, that they're a turn-on and it's okay to be turned on. "It may seem like I'd done this all along," Martin says, "but I really hadn't. I rarely felt the free choice to have sex or act out my fantasies in a spirit of playfulness. It always had the feeling of compulsion, like I had to *resort* to them. I was always, somehow, driven. And now I realize that the driven part comes from secretly hating myself, driving myself *against* myself. That was the resistance: I felt I had to fight myself in order to have sex, get pleasure, get what I wanted. I never realized I might simply deserve to have pleasure. That it was okay. That fantasies might not have to be so urgent. They might be something you decided to play with, or not play with, out of *choice*. This is radical news to me, that fantasies like mine aren't automatically pathological, that it might be okay just to accept them as a turn-on and leave it at that. Not that I can always have such an easygoing response to all this. I mean, they are primally connected to conflict. I know, in my heart, that I need to find more ways to deal with my anger than just through these fantasies. But the way out from under them, the way to lessen their urgency, isn't through fighting them. It's through accepting them, allowing them to be, giving them their due as turn-ons. I tell you, ever since I've had this new idea about them, that they might just be something to play with, they've sort of gone on the back burner. They don't tyrannize me so much anymore. In fact, last night one of my usual top men called me and said he wanted to get together and I said no, I was too tired, I just wasn't in the head for it. That's almost never happened before. Before I always thought I *had* to go through with it if someone asked me to. It didn't matter how tired I was, or whether or not I really wanted to have sex. God, it's been so long since I've known what it *is* to 'want' sex. I always have it so reflexively, I've lost touch with the hunger for it!" Martin lets out a surprised laugh. "More and more I've been feeling like, What was I so worried about? Why did I have so much fear? They're only fantasies. I don't have to do them if I don't want to!"

There's nothing wrong with fantasy being fantasy. It's only when we become convinced that fantasies are our only way out, or our only way of dealing with certain difficult feelings, that we get into trouble. Then we treat fantasies like we used to treat alcohol and drugs: as our only possible escape. Certainly if your sexual fantasies involve inflicting real psychological or physical harm to you or your partner, if you feel compelled to hurt yourself or someone else in the service of a fantasy, you may want to consider that the fantasy, like drinking or drugging, may be sabotaging you, hurting you more than helping you. This isn't to judge any fantasy, no matter how unconventional. It's merely a call to see if self-hate is the motive, rather than something that can involve a feeling of playfulness and self-love. How much is holding you back and increasing your fear, and how much is a more playful pleasure or exploration that you can choose to do or not do? No feelings or thoughts are off limits. We all have them, and we might as well accept that right off. It's only when we feel enslaved by our feelings and thoughts that we need to open our eyes, take a deep breath, and distance ourselves a bit to see where we are. The Twelve Steps are always there to help us do exactly that.

Martin strongly recommends getting professional help "when the fantasies become so unbearable that you can't imagine getting out from under them. Particularly when something like child abuse or incest is involved, we really need to reach out for all the help and reassurance we can find." But the automatic urge to hate a fantasy just because it is a fantasy doesn't seem to help much. Martin asks, "Why not enjoy it if you can?"

BLURRING SEX AND LOVE

One of the urgent desires fantasies exist to serve is the desire to make a *connection*. As convinced as Martin used to be that he had compartmentalized lust away from more aboveboard feelings of "romantic" love, when he began to explore his fantasies and the feelings attached to them, he had to admit that he had hopelessly confused lust and love all along. "This was maybe my biggest surprise," he says. "I see that the lust my sexual fantasies allowed me to feel was sort of me cutting to the chase, me getting quicker to the prize, the prize of orgasm, losing myself totally in a union with someone else. As much as I've always found love distasteful. It's always seemed sort of *feminine* and messy and uncontrollable—*needy*. I now see that some kind of love is what I've been after all along. I just don't know how to meet someone. Outside of the ritual of sadomasochistic sex, that is. But the real revelation is that it turns out I'm after something different than I thought I was. I even found myself saying to my own therapist the other day, 'What I don't need is more sex. What I need is more love.'"

Fantasies can be so consuming, so alluring, and so deceptive that they often blur our own perceptions of love and sex. But you may find yourself dealing with a dilemma opposite to Martin's. You may not start out thinking sex and love are different species of feeling; sex and love may be so inextricably bound that you can't help equating one with the other. Much in our culture encourages us to confuse the two.

Marika, forty-five and in NA for the past seven years, used to believe sex and love were the same thing. "In the late sixties and early seventies when the whole idea of free love hit everybody and it was suddenly get-into-as-many-beds-as-you-can time, I played around and slept with a bunch of different men. I tried to have it be cool that it was just sex, no strings, all that, but I could never help myself. Some man touched me and there was a part of me believed he knew my soul. How could someone be so physically close to you and not love you? I've never been able to understand it, separating sex from love."

Marika said she felt she was otherwise very much a product of her era and background. She prided herself on being one of the first black studies majors at a major university. "I had one impressive Afro," she laughs. "It was different back then, being black. You felt proud even in the ghetto. Different drugs, for one thing. Lot of heroin, of course, but also all those hallucinogens my friends and I did. It was more gentle; nobody was killing themselves on a crack high. We were college grads gone back up to Harlem to be with our people. I'm not sure who 'our people' were. They certainly weren't the family I left. I hated them. And most everybody else in the neighborhood thought we were weird snobs. We liked to think we were changing the world, but mostly we were getting high and quoting unknown African writers."

Marika thinks of her twenties and thirties as one long, blurred search for "something or someone perfect to take care of me forever. The something was usually a combination of marijuana, Tequila, and mescaline. The someone was whatever man it was politically correct and physically possible to get into bed with. And like I said, he'd just have to hold me naked in his arms and I couldn't believe, especially on all those drugs, that he didn't love me body and soul, forever. I kept thinking, when I was high and rolling around in a drugged-out vision with some man, This boy can see into my *soul*." Marika laughs uneasily. "God, what a fool I was. I just wish I'd stopped being a fool once I quit drugs."

In sobriety, Marika says she hasn't been able to let go of the fantasy that some "Prince Charming was going to descend from the sky and take me away from all this. And I haven't had much sex. Hell, I'm older, sober, afraid of AIDS, and frankly don't get much opportunity to go to bed with many men these days." She has hooked up with a few men who, in spite of some pretty hard evidence to the contrary, she can't go to bed with without thinking they'll save her. "Every one of them was married," she says. "I was in that classic thing of, It's just a matter of time before he realizes how much he loves me. He'll leave his wife and we'll go off and be artists in the South Pacific. Really, I'd do this to myself every time. It's getting exhausting. Every single one of them left me. But it was impossible for me to experience having sex with one of these men and not fall into the fantasy, once again, that he knew me to my very soul and would save me, as stupid as I know it sounds. I hate myself for it, but I can't stop it."

Being helplessly in love has become, to Marika, as bad a disease as her drug addiction ever was. "I've gone into therapy over it, but I'm so sick of talking about my abusive mother and my absent father. None of it is helping." What has helped, recently, is the growing sense that maybe she's got the power to give herself some of the "safety" she reflexively thinks she can only get from a man. "The last man I broke up with, Jack, told me the last night I saw him, 'You know, honey, whatever it is you want from me, I don't got. Maybe somebody got it, but I don't. Only I don't think you really know what you're after,' he said. 'You think you do, but I don't think you've really figured it out. And until you do, you're not going to get it. Simple as that.' Now Jack wasn't given to philosophizing, in fact that's the most I remember him saying to me in one night, but as I lay in my bed, lonely again, the next night, I began to wonder if what he said was true. This giant urge for somebody perfect, it was like the urge to get high. It had no darks and lights in it; I was just after some great blob of bliss. Some zonked-out state that was really more numb than happy but didn't admit any pain or fear. The problem was, that bliss wasn't *real*. It was then I began to see that my model for happiness, even all these years into sobriety, was still based on what I felt when I was high. On drugs I could bliss out and really convince myself the man I was with was my soul mate. I managed even in sobriety to keep the illusion going, but now it was starting to break down. For some reason, that night after the last time I saw Jack, I began to accept my aloneness a little more."

Marika says it was one of the most painful things she's done. "You know, I thought I'd been honest my whole life. And in sobriety, with my sponsor, my sponsees, and talking in meetings, I had a reputation for letting it all hang out. My sponsor sometimes tells me she wishes I'd keep a little more of it *in*," Marika laughs. "But I hadn't faced something central in me, hadn't faced it at all. It was that I was terrified of being alone. When I had any kind of romantic or sexual contact, it activated the love button, the bliss button, and I turned whoever it was into the perfect soul mate I was so desperate to meet. He turned into love because I was so hungry for love, I'd imagine it even if it wasn't there. I needed to face some new facts and feelings about myself: perfect love would never just happen automatically in every man I met, but it was okay to *want* love and to acknowledge that I wanted it and didn't have it. It was okay to admit I was in pain, that I was needy. I didn't have to rush out and fill the void like I used to do when I got high. I could live with the pain, maybe learn from it. I could survive it."

The idea that we can survive our feelings is a shocking one to every recovering alcoholic and addict I've ever met. We became conditioned to respond to certain cues by turning to alcohol or drugs, which created and reinforced the idea of a reward system: whenever you felt distress, or joy, or any emotion at all, you could "fix" it or "reward" yourself by getting high. Emotion equaled action. You felt something? You grabbed for something to get rid of the feeling, to control it, manage it, bury it, make it behave. Elation, anger, or depression—whatever stimulated us in some sense frightened us; it was beyond our control. And so we grabbed for something to control it, either to enhance it to the point of impervious pleasure so that pain was not even a possibility, or to swamp it, kill it, steamroll it into numbness so we wouldn't have to feel anything at all. For many of us this state of numbness was the state to which we most aspired. And, for many of us, we only stopped drinking and drugging when it couldn't reliably bring us to that numbness, when nothing we did could keep away the pain any more.

In recovery, as happily free as we may be of the damage that drugs and alcohol caused us, we are also, often less happily, just as free of the escape they afforded us. It takes time before the idea of the simplistic reward system we reinforced when we drank or drugged gives way to something more useful, more satisfying. For a very long time, we may grab for food or money or sex as a replacement for the "reward" we gave up when we stopped getting high. Marika knows now that that's why she kept ballooning any contact she had with a man into "some version of the ultimate prize. I thought I always had to *have* an ultimate prize. I couldn't just be with someone and let him be who he was. I had to turn him into the perfect solution. Which is really a stand-in for the perfect high. Facing reality isn't something I'm used to doing."

Reality is rounder than most of us are comfortable admitting. Pain is part of it, as are moments of sorrow and boredom and anger. But so are wonder and curiosity and joy. The people you've met in this chapter, and in this book as a whole, are all in the process of apprehending this larger, more encompassing sense of reality, and one of the dividends they're experiencing in the sexual and romantic realm is that they're slowly developing a clearer idea of what sex and romance *mean* to each of them. We've seen that our sexual fantasies can teach us a great deal about the meaning we've learned to attach to lust and love. We've learned that we can survive looking at our fantasies, and that they can survive being coaxed out into the light. Sometimes we discover that the fantasies we thought we hated, we don't hate. Like Martin, we may allow ourselves to enjoy them as we develop a more playful sense of choice in integrating them into our emotional and sexual lives. Sometimes, as with Marika, we may see the haze they create and learn, slowly, to discern more clearly what that haze is obscuring. "Sex is not the same thing as love," is one of Marika's findings, as she's allowed herself to peer through the haze.

"Maybe it's all right to acknowledge my need for love and be more patient with myself" is another. Grace, along with Marika and Martin, has developed a rich appreciation of how ingeniously self-protective fantasies are; she is learning to respect the fact that they deserve compassionate attention, not contempt.

"You cannot have too much compassion for yourself," Grace says her sponsor keeps telling her. She smiles ruefully: "Imagine that! I used to think you couldn't have too little."

CHAPTER 5

Bodies (and Souls): The Physical You

Okay, turn on the light, take off your clothes and look at yourself in a full-length mirror. Come on, keep your eyes open.

Facing and accepting who we are physically is highly charged territory. We often manifest our shaky senses of self by hating our bodies, how we look, by not being able even to imagine anyone finding us attractive. "I have a hard time accepting compliments about anything," one young recovering woman says, "but I especially don't believe anyone who says I look good. I always feel they have some ulterior motive or maybe some fetish about my red hair. They couldn't really be complimenting *me*. If they only knew how imperfect I looked, how fat my thighs are, for instance! It's so hard for me to take my clothes off in front of anyone, even my doctor."

This volatile territory brings us face to face with the bedrock of how we feel about ourselves. Recovering people have taught me something I now believe is axiomatic: how you feel about your body is a direct reflection of how you feel about the inner you, who you perceive yourself "really" to be. This doesn't mean that if you don't think you're gorgeous all the time you've got a problem. It means addressing an issue that is at the root of hating how you look: self-esteem. Addicts and alcoholics are expert at escaping feelings. Sometimes it is a trial to even accept that we *exist* physically: "I only look at certain parts of me when I pass a mirror," says one recovering alcoholic; "I've trained my eyes to stay away from my waist-line. It would be too devastating!" says another. This separation from our bodies is why many alcoholics and addicts, even in sobriety, are reluctant to go to the doctor or the dentist. Waking up to who you are physically and accepting, even eventually loving, what you find seems to be an essential part of the self-discovery of sobriety.

People's experience of their physical selves offers clues about how we might go about understanding and improving our body esteem.

The Tyranny of Body Image

You'd never know it to look at him, but Ben, a twenty-six-year-old finely chiseled bodybuilder who's been sober in AA for the past three years, used to be fat. "I was about fifty pounds overweight all through junior high and high school," Ben says. "People would make fun of me. Even now when I hear some-one shout out, 'Hey, fatso!' I look up. Fatso was my middle name." Ben now has the idea that he overate for much the same reasons that he ended up drinking: "to escape. My par-ents were like Greek gods to me. About as distant as gods, too. They were beautiful. My mother used to be a model, and my father is this real handsome business executive. Sort of a model couple. At least on the outside. They ended up divorc-ing when I was thirteen, which I think just got me to eat more, the anxiety of it. I went through my adolescence in a severe state of withdrawal. My only comfort was food. I stayed with my mother after the divorce, almost never saw my father. But my mother was so self-absorbed, going out with a lot of men; she didn't have much time for me. I was a lonely fat kid. That was pretty much my whole story."

Ben chose to go to a college on the East Coast, thousands of miles away from where he'd grown up on the West Coast. "I figured, maybe I could reinvent myself if I went far enough away. If I met people who didn't know who I was, maybe I could be a whole different person. I had a lot of fantasies of changing my name, lying about my background, creating a whole new story about myself. Getting away from home was the thing I wanted to do most of all. In fact, that was my solution to everything: get away from it!" Excited by the prospect of living in a new place, Ben found himself wanting not to eat so much. "If I was going to be a new person, maybe I didn't have to be such a *fat* new person." The idea even occurred to him that he might want to exercise a little. "My father had left some barbells down in the basement, and I'd sneak down there to play around with them when my mother wasn't around." He noticed some differences early on. "I actually grew some biceps," he says. "It dawned on me: maybe I didn't just have to fantasize about being a new person. Maybe I actually had some control over how I looked!"

That was the beginning, Ben says, of his bodybuilding obsession. "When I got to college, I was already hooked. First thing I did was check out the gym to see what kind of equipment they had. They had Nautilus machines, which I'd been dying to try. I drummed up my courage and asked an assistant coach to teach me about how to use them. He did. And that was it. You wanted to find me, I was at the gym." Ben said that working out felt like "staging an all-out attack on the fat boy I used to be. I was like the worst sort of army commander. I didn't allow myself any slack. If I missed a workout, I went through agony. I remember once I got the flu and I was so weak I could barely walk down the hill to the gym, but I did anyway. When I tried to work out on one of the machines and was too weak to do it, I actually cried right there, like a baby. I grabbed onto working out and changing my body like a life raft. There was nothing else that could save me. If I stopped for any amount of time, I was afraid I'd turn back into jelly. Being this new me required constant vigilance."

Ben was a couple of years into college when he realized he could get some relief from his anxiety-ridden regime by drinking. "I stuck to hard stuff because I got it into my head that beer would put fat on me, but vodka and whisky wouldn't. I don't know why I thought that. Hard liquor has a lot of empty calories, just like beer. But that's what I decided." Ben hated the taste of liquor at first, but he liked the relaxation it gave him, and it became as regular for him to get bombed every night as it did to work out every day. "I was on a pretty steep downhill track," he says. "Workouts got harder because of the awful hangovers. But now I couldn't stop—didn't want to stop—drinking, and I just disciplined myself more to work out even when my head felt like someone was splitting atoms in it." Ben's school work, to which he'd only ever paid minimal attention, soon got ignored completely. "Eventually I dropped out of college. All I wanted to do was work out and drink. I didn't go out with girls much, even though by this time people thought of me as a pretty good-looking guy. I was as wrapped into myself and afraid of people as I'd ever been back in high school when I was fat and unpopular. I got a job at a supermarket in the college town, lived in a single-room-only hotel, and worked out an arrangement with the assistant coach to keep using the Nautilus equipment. But I was heading down real fast." Ben was so hung over and sick one day that he threw up and passed out in the gym. "It was the humiliation of it that got to me. I felt so completely out of control, and here were all these college guys picking me up off the floor, me lying in a pool of vomit. I was supposed to be this big strong guy, right? Jesus."

Because he didn't want to give up working out, Ben finally decided to get some help with what he know knew was a drinking problem. He started attending some AA meetings he knew were held every week on campus. Something about the idea of sobriety appealed to him. He stopped drinking. The physical improvement was almost instantaneous: no more headaches and he slept better. His old physical energy come back. "But before long the anxiety came back too. I was just as obsessed about my body as I ever was before. Only now, in some ways, it was worse. Before, at least, booze allowed me to check out and not have to deal with my loneliness. I tried to make my workouts blot all this out and became more and more obsessive. But I couldn't get away from the pain." Ben began to wonder who it was he was making himself into an Adonis for. "I'd gone out on some dates, like to frat parties in college, and even went to bed with a couple women, always drunk. But I felt so awkward. I preferred fantasizing about sex to actually having it. Sometimes I'd get pornography and get off on that. Though, God knows, I *looked* at enough women. In fact, I had, still have, this automatic rating system for how people look, just like some kind of school report card. I've never been able to get above about a B plus or an A minus myself. And I've never been able to go out with a woman I thought was higher up on the rating scale than I was. The few times I've been to bed with a woman, I had to make sure I felt she wasn't any higher than B or B plus. I don't think I could have functioned if I thought she was better off than I was in that regard. It sounds stupid, doesn't it? But that's how I feel."

In AA, after about a year, Ben became very interested in a woman named Beth, who was his age and had the same amount of time in the program he had. "I liked her because she seemed to be as driven as I was. She talked about being addicted to running. How she'd beat herself up if she missed a day. I identified with that, obviously. But she scared me in another way. Beth was a solid A plus on the looks scale. She freaked me out. She looked like a dancer. Not an ounce of fat on her. Like this sensuous cat or something. So beautiful, graceful. I felt like such a lunk around her. Whenever I saw her it always suddenly reminded me of this little band of fat I've never been able to lose around my waist. I just felt stupid, clumsy, and fat around her. There's something else that's harder to admit. Every time I begin to fantasize about having sex with Beth, I feel humiliated. I'm not exactly, er . . . super-endowed. The cliché about how bodybuilders build huge muscles to make up for not having a big you-know-what? Well, I'm afraid I fit that model. I mean, I feel inadequate pretty much all around. And with Beth, the bottom line was I couldn't imagine that she'd ever want to pay attention to me."

Ben was surprised, therefore, when Beth approached him after an AA meeting and asked if he'd like to go out to coffee. "She seemed real nervous," Ben says. "I couldn't imagine why. I mean, didn't she realize she had the upper hand? Didn't she realize how beautiful she was, how superior she was to me?" Evidently Beth had quite a different view of herself. "She really cut to the chase, once we'd gotten to the coffee shop and sat down. She just blurted out how intimidated she felt around

me, that I was such a big strong athletic man and seemed so se-
cure about it, and how did I manage to get all this self-esteem?
She was really worried. She was miserable. She was afraid she
was anorexic. She was morbidly afraid that if she ate anything
other than an occasional leaf of lettuce she'd turn into a
blimp. Her anxiety was getting so great she was afraid she
might go out and drink. She talked to her sponsor about it, but
her sponsor didn't know what it was like to drive yourself
physically the way she did. So she thought if she talked to me,
because she knew I was so into working out and taking care of
my body, maybe I'd have some clues about how to let up on
herself, how to calm down. 'How do you get self-esteem?' is
what she kept asking again and again. What did I know that
she didn't?"

Ben was floored. "But I decided to go for broke, since she
had. I was more honest than I ever thought I could be. I ad-
mitted that I was equally intimidated by her. I even told her
about my rating system and how she had totally aced it. I
couldn't imagine her feeling bad about herself. It amazed me.
We both looked at each other for a moment like we'd come
from different planets. How could we each have the self-view
we had? From her point of view, I had made it! From my point
of view, she was a goddess!" Ben shakes his head. "After a moment of shocked silence, we just burst out laughing."

It was a helpful meeting for both of them. "That thing
about not judging someone else's outsides by your insides: it
sure applied to us. I'm not saying that I magically think I'm so
terrific now that this beautiful woman has complimented me.
And I don't think she's solved her low self-esteem problem by
hearing that I think she looks terrific. Not that we didn't get
off on each other's compliments. Another thing that's true of
both her and me is something you hear a lot in the rooms: how

the pendulum swings between grandiosity, thinking you're the greatest thing in the world, to feeling like a slug, thinking you're the worst. Both of us, Beth and I, *crave* to believe that we're physical paragons, that we could get to a state of perfection where we'd never have to worry about not being attractive, where we'd just automatically attract the people we wanted to attract, where we'd be lovable, where we'd be *okay*. But when I talked about this conversation with my sponsor the next day, I realized how *sad* it is that we feel such a huge hunger to feel that nth degree of safety, okayness. We had to be perfect to be marginally acceptable; that's what it really boiled down to. God, it's exhausting to live like that. I really needed help, and I knew Beth did too."

That need for help has brought Ben more strongly back to the program. "I realized how healing the process of the Steps is. How it really encourages us not only to be kind to ourselves, but also to put the emphasis on what we can give to the world, not what we can squeeze out of it. I know on some deeper level that I have to shift the direction my energy is going, from obsessively inward to a more gentle flow outward. Talking to Beth was a real revelation. I saw what a help it was simply to be there and listen. And it drained the whole intimidation thing right out of me. She is a hurting human being, just like me. Just as vulnerable, even as fallible, as I am. I find that when I allow my heart to go out to someone, I also allow it to go out to me. When I feel real compassion for someone else, the way I do now for Beth, it seems to open up my capacity for feeling better about myself."

Ben says he's also begun talking to other bodybuilders about his anxieties. "I just always expected other guys were totally together about all this. But I have this gym buddy, and I decided to tell him a little about my own nutsiness about working out, how being so driven made me feel. It was amazing. I mean, as far as I know this guy isn't even in recovery. But it was like a dam burst. He was so grateful to get an opening to talk about his own fear and anxiety! Now we joke about getting a support group together: Bodybuilders Anonymous."

A welcome dividend of facing our shame, anxiety, and fear seems to be that we find we can *enjoy* ourselves more. "Now that I'm starting to let up on myself a little," Ben says, "I'm actually enjoying my workouts more than I used to. I guess it's because I feel a tiny bit less driven. Like I'm actually choosing to do this, not like I have to do it. Okay, it's still pretty much of an obsession to me. But when I talk to my gym buddy, I seem to be able to laugh a little about it. It's not all so damned serious. And that's letting me have some fun. I can't tell you how different that is. I never allowed myself to have *fun* before. That was unthinkable, that I might actually enjoy something!" Ben laughs again, clearly enjoying something right now.

THE BONDAGE OF SELF-DISGUST

Who you feel yourself to be inside is often considerably different from how you're perceived by others. Ben says, "I realize now that I don't have any control over somebody else's opinion of me. I mean, if Beth had reacted the way I thought she would, she wouldn't have given me the time of day! And if I'd reacted to her the way *she* thought I was going to, I wouldn't have agreed to talk to her. I'd be too disgusted by how ugly she was. We're really nut cases about ourselves, about how we project we're coming across."

However, many (if not most) of us don't have Ben and Beth's problem of accepting how muscular and svelte our bodies are. Our physical imperfections are all too evident for us ever to imagine that we might give Mr. or Ms. Universe a bad night's sleep. Some of us are fat. Some of us have wrinkles, bad teeth, sagging jowls. Some of us battle far more debilitating circumstances: a mastectomy, a missing leg or arm, AIDS, multiple sclerosis, cancer, heart disease—any number of physical disabilities. It's safe to say that by culturally received standards of physical beauty and health, standards that are pounded into us every time we read a magazine or turn on the television and see a soap opera or a beer ad, the majority of us find ourselves lacking. Given the shaky self-esteem most people in recovery often experience, these perceived "lacks" can be devastating.

Marilyn says that she's fat and she knows it. "I've tried to play the jolly fat person. I've tried to do a lot of things to make up for not being most people's idea of an ideal beautiful woman." Marilyn used to avoid facing her physical imperfections through drugs. "Pot, mostly. That would calm me down, let me erase reality, let me forget, really, that I even had a physical body! But to really check out, for special occasions, like every weekend, I'd also do hallucinogens like mescaline." Marilyn lives in the Haight district of San Francisco even though, at thirty, she's too young to have known it in its 1968 hippie heyday. "I feel like I was born too late, like I missed out on my real era. I'm living in the one place on earth where I can pretend I'm still in that era, but it still feels like I've missed the boat."

Freaking out one too many times on hallucinogens is what eventually got Marilyn into NA. "They were making me paranoid. I used to enjoy feeling like I'd left the planet, but at the end I felt I was going to hell, not to some suburb of Nirvana. I'd moved from mescaline to heavy doses of LSD. I imagined horrible crawling things were on my skin. Plants turned into flesh-eating monsters. The walls trembled and oozed blood. It was like tripping had unleashed the worst my head could do to me. I started to be terribly afraid, even when I didn't do drugs. The horrible dark reality I'd clued into on drugs was still there. It was trying to get out, banging like some horrible creature against a door I wasn't sure could stay locked." Marilyn went into therapy and decided to take her therapist's suggestion to go to NA. "I felt at home for the first time in my life," she says. "I actually met people who'd felt as paranoid as I had, and I can't tell you how much it's helped to connect with them. I just don't feel so alone any more. But another result of all this isn't so great. I find I can no longer escape my body. I keep remembering I *have* one. Which is not a pleasant experience."

Marilyn hadn't had a physical exam since she was a little girl in school. "I'd been having sharp pains in my side, but I was too scared and too humiliated at the thought of anyone, even a doctor, poking and prodding my fat body for me to make an appointment. So I'd just try to wish the pain away. I also did a lot of meditation, trying to tell myself I was doing the eleventh Step, the one about seeking through prayer and meditation to establish more contact with my Higher Power. I've been into a lot of New Age stuff, especially the idea that all illness is caused by some misalignment of the spirit and if you work on the spirit you can cure the body. But I never really believed that. I just clung to it to block out how afraid I was that these pains in my side meant I had cancer or something. I was desperate to find some mind game I could get into to escape, once again, the fact that I was a physical being."

One of her New Age seminars ended up backfiring, however. "My sponsor, who's into the same spiritual type of stuff

I'm into, invited me to go with her to a meditation seminar that had to do with healing shame. That sounded good to me. God knows, shame is something I've been grappling with my whole life! So I said yes pretty eagerly. But if I'd known what was going to happen, I wouldn't have been so eager.

"I thought it was going to be this guided meditation thing where you didn't have to do anything but sit in a chair and close your eyes and drift away thinking about the beach or the forest. But the leader of the seminar said that he wanted us to do some yoga thing as part of the meditation. I freaked. I've avoided anything that involves moving my limbs in any way. It all just seems like gym class, and, God, I had such humiliating memories of gym class back in school! I literally broke into a sweat and was about to leave the room. But I was in the front row, and I also have a horror of drawing attention to myself, which I would have done in spades by getting up and walking the whole length of the room to get out. I was stuck. I decided that the lesser of the two evils was to go through with it. But, oh! It was agony . . . "

Marilyn miserably resigned herself to following the group leader's instructions. "We had to lie on the floor, which at least was carpeted. I was so tense! I was sure he was going to make us twist ourselves into pretzels. My side started to ache. I felt like I had to go to the bathroom, even though I'd just been before the seminar had started. I closed my eyes and asked my Higher Power for strength." Marilyn was happily surprised, however, by what the group leader told them to do next. "He said all we had to do was gently rock our heads just barely from side to side, feeling the slight pull in our necks, imagining that we were moving our heads like we'd rock a sleeping infant. Then he asked us to go down a bit and rock our shoulders back and forth, just as gently, no abrupt movements, softly side to side, with the same idea that we were rhythmically rocking a baby. He wanted us to feel the muscles in our necks and shoulders, not do anything about them, just feel them. We then rocked our torsos gently back and forth, and then our hips and legs. It was all so slow and gentle and nonthreatening. And, incredibly, it felt wonderful! Until . . . " Marilyn's eyes, which had closed as she recited all this, suddenly opened. "It was wonderful until he asked us to go back in time and call up any shame or humiliation we'd felt about our bodies so that we could begin to face and heal it. Some terrible things came up for me. It was almost like I was tripping again! Like the door I'd so carefully kept locked suddenly burst open. Being made fun of as a little girl by the neighborhood kids. Not having any friends. My mother keeping me home from the beach because she was ashamed of how I looked in a bathing suit. And then, closer to the present, stuff to do with sex. This humiliating time when I was at a party, stoned out of my mind, feeling full of peace and love and druggy bliss, thinking the whole world finally loved me unconditionally, and this guy walks by, looks down on me, and whispers to his friend, thinking I couldn't hear him, 'Ugh! Imagine going to bed with *her?*'" Marilyn starts to cry, which she did then too. "I felt such *shame.* You think I'm crying now? I was sobbing in the seminar. It was so bad that people around me started to reach out and touch my hands, tried to hold me and comfort me. At first I shook them off, angrily. I didn't want anyone to touch me, not then, not ever! But then I just gave in. Something in me just released. And I let myself be comforted. Slowly, I came back and up from all that shame and returned to the present. I felt flattened, like all the energy and air had gone out of me, but better. The pressure was less. Something in me was at least a little less tight."

Marilyn says she was glad her sponsor was there. "I needed to sort out these feelings with someone I trusted, and my sponsor was such a help. After the seminar we went for a long walk through Golden Gate Park. It was a beautiful late afternoon. We talked about program stuff: how facing all of that horrible shame turned out not to be as dangerous as I was always afraid it would be. And I didn't have to face any of it alone. I could let it out and talk about it. It was the kind of thing I heard all the time in NA meetings: turning it over, reaching out for help, all of that. But I'd never really allowed myself to loosen and trust that I could 'let it all out' myself. Now I'd found out I could."

When Marilyn went to bed that night she found herself reliving the same shameful memories she'd had in the seminar but in a different way. "I felt a little more distant from them. They didn't frighten me so much. It was like they'd lost their power over me. I found I was somehow more *curious* about their effect on me. I wanted to know more about where my fears came from. It felt like I had at least made a start, and I was glad. But then, as if to remind me to pay attention to problems I was facing right then and there, I felt a little twinge in my side. The old fear came up again. There was that mysterious pain. I wanted to escape it, block it out, ignore it! But, for the first time, I didn't let myself run away. I felt the pain. And I made the decision, right then, to call a doctor the next day and make an appointment. I suddenly *wanted* to. That was the difference. There was just less fear about it. I don't know where this capacity came from, but I suddenly believed what I'd always heard in the rooms: that God wouldn't give me anything I couldn't handle. There was no reason to fear anything. I could trust, just like I'd been able to trust my sponsor and the people at that seminar. Someone, something would catch me. I wouldn't fall."

Marilyn did go to the doctor and was relieved. The pains in her side were caused by a mild case of diverticulosis, not cancer as she'd secretly feared, and she could take care of the problem by changing her diet. "The very word *diet* was so scary to me," Marilyn says, smiling a little. "And here I was talking with the doctor about a new diet as if it were the most normal and least threatening thing in the world! He outlined a plan for me that I could follow not only to get rid of my diverticulosis but maybe even lose some weight." Marilyn sighs. "You can't know how amazing this is, facing this stuff, taking these actions to take care of myself . . . I feel like I'm here, in this world, in a way I've never felt before. Like I don't have to hide quite so much. And although it's still no great treat to look at myself in a mirror, I don't wince quite so badly. I don't *hate* what I see. I even find myself wondering, down the line, if I might hook up with a man. It doesn't seem so outlandish to me that someone might want to be with me. That's still in the fantasy stage. But even allowing the barest glimmer of that possibility in—well, it's a miracle."

THE COURAGE TO TAKE A BUBBLE BATH

Irene, married with three kids and living in what she calls "a typical suburban split level" in New Jersey, has what appears to be a very different background and sense of herself than Marilyn, but she's grappling with a lot of the same self-mistrust. The breakthrough she came to, which happened in the midst of taking a bubble bath, also felt like a miracle to her.

Irene knows she looks "pared down." "You should see my family pictures. Every one of us looks like something out of that Grant Wood picture, that dour couple with a pitchfork on the farm, gaunt and humorless. We're skinny and withdrawn. It's like it's a genetic trait." Thinking back to her childhood is something Irene's sponsor has been encouraging her to do lately. "I've been sober in AA for nearly six years now, but it was only these past couple of months that I could bring myself to doing a fourth Step. I've known all my life that there were memories I just didn't want to face. And frankly, I never understood why I had to face them; it just seemed like picking at old wounds. The one part of the program I clung to like a life raft, at least about my memories, was 'Let go, let God.' What I now realize I meant by that was 'Let me ignore all this. I'm too afraid to face it.' I'm finally learning that 'turning it over' doesn't mean blocking it out and running away from it. It's a subtle distinction for a lot of recovering alcoholics and addicts, I think. Calling on spiritual help to give you strength doesn't mean looking for some Great White Father to do everything for you, make it all better. It doesn't mean absolving ourselves of all responsibility . . . "

Irene is now able to talk about some of what she used to block herself from looking at. "I grew up in Nebraska on a farm. I had six brothers who did all the work, starting as soon as they could walk just about. My father was all work and no play. I really think the reason he got married was to have a slew of kids to use as a work force on the farm. It was like having a built-in farm crew: when you needed someone else, you had another baby. Standards were very traditional. I was supposed to take care of the house because I was a girl. My father was thrilled he'd had so many sons. I don't think he would have known what to do with as many girls as he had boys. It was unthinkable to him that a girl might be able to plow a field. I was supposed to stay in the house and cook and clean." For Irene, staying in the house mostly meant one thing: taking care of her mother. "My mother was delicate. She kept having babies and surviving the births, but just barely. Each birth made her weaker. I'm the second youngest. She was very sick after she had me, and a year and a half later, she hemorrhaged and nearly died giving birth to my little brother. The doctor finally convinced my father to stop impregnating her." Irene shakes her head. "We lived on a farm, remember. It was all pretty direct. Like keeping a bull away from a cow so the cow wouldn't have any more calves. My father was a pragmatic man. I don't think sex was something he thought about except as a way to produce more offspring. If he couldn't have it, well, that's just the way it was. How my mother felt about it I don't know. She was such an unhappy woman and so out of it most of the time I don't know what she felt, whether she missed sleeping with my father or if she was just too far gone to care anymore."

Irene now realizes her mother was severely emotionally disturbed as well as a closet alcoholic. "She would stock up on cough medicine mostly. She always had a cough or could 'feel one coming on.' She'd had pneumonia when I was about six years old, and it nearly killed her. So she was hyperconcerned about it ever coming back. The most important thing in her life was making sure she had enough medicine. When she managed to come down for breakfast, she'd fumble around with pots and pans and look so inept and then start coughing that even my father would feel sorry for her. 'Go back to bed, honey,' he'd say. They were the kindest words I ever heard him say, certainly the only time I'd ever heard him say 'honey.' Anyway, she would make a show of resistance, then gratefully go back upstairs. And chug some more cough medicine."

Irene closes her eyes. "Nobody but me knew what was really going on. Since I was the only one taking care of the house—my brothers and my father were always out in the fields except for meals—I was stuck with the incredible mess my mother made of herself. By the time I was about twelve or thirteen, it was like I'd turned into the mother. She would pass out from her medicine. She'd wet the bed and sometimes throw up or have diarrhea. God, I shudder to remember it now. I dreaded going into her bedroom to check up on her. I spent my childhood cleaning up my mother. And I mean down to the skin, all over. But the real effect, I'm now beginning to see, is that I started to be disgusted by the human body. And not only hers. Mine. And, later, my husband's."

Irene's mother died when Irene was nineteen. "It was a year after I'd graduated from high school. It never occurred to me until my mother died that I ever had the right to leave the farm. But I can't tell you the relief I felt. I think all my family did. It was like some great black presence had been removed from the house. I feel so sorry for her sometimes, realizing how much everyone just wanted her to die. But she was such a miserable woman, and I couldn't pretend I missed her. I didn't. And it gave me permission to get the hell out of the house: out of the farm, the state, and across the country. I'd always had this secret desire to do something literary. Not even write especially, just teach English. I lived on the books I borrowed from the county library we'd go to every month. It was my only escape. I read all of Jane Austen, over and over; everyone spoke so beautifully, dressed so prettily. Could there really have been a world like that, so delicate and beautiful? I fled to these books after cleaning up my mother's urine or feces or pushing her back up into bed after she'd fallen out of it. It was such a contrast."

Irene ended up in New Jersey near New York City, a city she thought of as some kind of compelling but slightly sinister Oz. "Manhattan scared me. It was exhilarating to be so near somewhere that big and exciting, but it was a long time before

I could drum up the courage to take the train in and do anything there. I didn't think I could handle it. All I'd ever known was a farm in Nebraska. So I lived in a middle-sized town in New Jersey near enough to the city to convince myself I could feel its energy. It was a strange time. I got a job in a department store in a shopping mall and started taking night courses at a local community college. I wanted to be a teacher. That's when I met my husband. Frank was a teacher in the college. Not an English teacher; he taught chemistry, of all things. I couldn't imagine what any of that was about. But he took an interest in me. He liked the idea that I was a farm girl who loved Jane Austen. I was very careful to speak well, a stickler for grammar. He was precise in his own ways. We started going out, and a couple of months later he asked me to marry him. I did. No one had ever paid attention to me the way Frank did. I don't know that I was in love; I was just so grateful to him for noticing me, for wanting me. It seemed unbelievable. Ever since I'd moved to the East Coast, I'd felt invisible. Frank made me think I was actually *there*."

It was after she got married that Irene started drinking. "It was really about sex. It was terrible, but I totally shut down every time Frank touched me. We went to Florida for our honeymoon, and the first night, when he got into bed with me naked, I actually started to tremble and then cry. *I didn't want him to touch me*. He was very gentle, though. He seemed to understand. The hotel we were staying at had given us a couple of bottles of champagne. We were on a honeymoon package, and champagne was included. Frank got up out of bed, put on a robe, and opened a bottle. He almost never drank, and I had literally never tasted alcohol in my life. I was so paranoid about what happened to my mother with her cough syrup that I didn't want to get near anything that might play with my head. But I drank the champagne. In fact, I ended up drinking most of the bottle. It was wonderful. For the first time in my life, I had the feeling of really letting go. Things just weren't so serious anymore! I felt like I could handle anything. There was no reason to fear. Frank took me to bed, and I let him slip off my nightgown. He took off his robe and turned out the light. When he touched me, it was like it was happening to someone else. Like I had turned into this acquiescent rag doll and it didn't matter who did what to it because there was no feeling. Just a kind of distant, slightly pleasant numbness. When he entered me, it was like I was a million miles away; I didn't feel anything. I was vaguely curious about it, sort of like looking at farm animals coupling, but there was no emotion, none at all."

This pretty much set the pattern for Irene's sex life for the next ten years. She could only have sex with Frank if she'd had a lot to drink. What began to change, however, was that she began to need to drink at other times as well. "We had our first child, Billy, about two years after we were married. Sally came two years later; Jim, right on schedule two years after that. I'd had to drop out of college when Billy was born. It was just too much work having a little baby. But it was something more than that too. As I got more and more buried in housework again, the old me, the me who was chained to my parents' house and to my mother's sickness, seemed to come out again. I started feeling numb about everything. I just went through the motions. Almost like a robot. It's not that I didn't love Billy and then my other two kids. But every time I played mother, it was as if I had to tell some essential central part of me to go to sleep. I had to bring out the robot, the caretaker, the one who could fix everything. The feeling me just got buried deeper and deeper. I know I was feeling a lot of anger too. I resented the fact that I couldn't have my own life, spend my time reading wonderful novels, then maybe teaching or even writing. All of those aspirations had been shot to hell. Sometimes, although pretty rarely, I'd blow up out of nowhere and scare Frank and my kids out of their wits. By the time Jim was born, I was drinking pretty heavily. Always on the sly. I'd sneak out of bed after everyone was asleep, go down to the kitchen, and start drinking brandy. When I was sufficiently steamrolled by that, I'd stumble to the bathroom, gargle with mouthwash, and go back to bed. I had to escape somehow. Those late-night, early-morning binges were the only time I could get away and be myself. Except it never felt like it was myself I was being. It felt like I was trying, desperately, by drinking enough, to keep whatever self I had down and out of sight. Keep tightening the lid. Get away! That's what I kept saying to myself really."

After one of these late-night binges, Irene decided that she didn't want to go back to bed with Frank. She remembers being very drunk. "I looked at a kitchen knife that I'd left out on the countertop. It suddenly seemed completely rational to take the knife and cut my wrists. I actually picked the thing up with my right hand and held the blade over my left wrist. I let the blade go down and touch my skin. I could feel its sharp edge and remember thinking how easy it would be to jerk the knife down deeper into me. Suddenly it was as if some part of me, maybe the me I'd been trying so hard to push down, rose up from the depths, shot out up above me, and looked down at what I was doing. I saw myself sitting there, drunk, about to cut my own flesh. I was horrified. What was I doing? I don't know where it came from, but I had this sudden overwhelming feeling that I wanted to live. It was amazing. You talk about a spiritual awakening, I guess that was mine. I started to sob. So loud that Frank was awakened and came into the kitchen. By that time I'd put down the knife so he didn't realize what I'd just been about to do. He asked me what was wrong. I blubbered at him, 'I've decided I want to live.' He was so sleepy and my speech was so slurred, he didn't have any idea what I'd said. 'Well, why don't you come back to bed and sleep on it,' he finally said. 'See if you feel the same way tomorrow.' In the middle of my crying, I started to laugh, which *completely* bewildered poor Frank."

When Irene woke up she decided she wanted to go to a therapist, and she found one through a clinic in the Yellow Pages, which also happened to have an outpatient drug and alcohol rehabilitation program. All this led her to AA. "I hated AA at first. All those people talking about their secrets so openly in a group. That was about as far from what I thought I was capable of doing as you could get. But slowly I made some friends, and I could begin to make my own peace with the program. I began to realize that the Twelve Steps only make sense when you can find a way to have them make sense to *you*. I got a sponsor early on, a sweet matronly grandmother who's still my sponsor now all these years later. She was so gentle with me, so accepting, that I began to ease up a bit."

Physical sobriety was a surprise to Irene. "I'd blocked out feeling anything for so long that I never acknowledged I'd ever had a hangover. I just ignored pain, wouldn't admit it was there. But now that I was no longer drinking and was sleeping better and feeling so much better in the morning, I realized my whole life for ten years had been a hangover. I'd never known anything else!" However, this new clarity had a down side. "Now that I was so much more aware of my surroundings and how I felt, it scared me. I started to get paranoid about things. Almost like Howard Hughes, when I think of it. Suddenly I worried about germs. I worried about my kids going to school and catching some horrible disease and dying. I got obsessive about keeping things clean and hygienic. I couldn't abide any disorder, which, in a house with three little kids, is pretty much a losing proposition. I began to blow up like I'd never blown up before. Sobriety had unleashed feelings, anger and fears, in me I never knew were there. And sex just stopped altogether. Every time Frank made a sexual overture, I panicked. All I could think of was the physical aspects of it, the dirtiness, the body fluids, the sweat, the ugliness. Like squashing a bunch of chicken gizzards together. This was supposed to be pleasure? Why would anyone want to do it?"

Irene would plead headache after headache. "It was awful. I dreaded the moment we'd both go to bed. I couldn't bear to be near him. There was just something so horrible about naked flesh to me! And I know Frank was really hurt. In some ways he was just as blocked about facing and talking about his feelings as I was, which I was glad about because I didn't think I could handle hearing about them! I felt so guilty. I was not living up to my wifely obligations; that's what kept coming up for me. Eventually, sooner and sooner each night, he'd just turn over and go to sleep. In a few years we were at completely opposite sides of the bed, our backs to each other. But I couldn't bear it any other way. We were miserable; we couldn't talk about it, but I couldn't imagine it ever changing."

Irene says it was about this time that the nightmares started. "They were all about the body, my body. My teeth would start to crumble and fall out, and I'd keep trying to push them back in and not have anyone know I was disintegrating. Or this terrible body smell would come out, and I'd realize with horror that it was coming out of me! These were such frightening, shameful dreams. I'd wake up terrified." Irene began to talk about them with her sponsor. "My sponsor was wonderful. She just let me speak, didn't offer any dime store psychologizing. She just knew I had to let this out in whatever ways and however long I needed. And finally, a few months ago, I got to the real shame, the real source of all this. I had a dream about my body sort of moldering in bed, the skin all soft and flabby and falling off my bones, making a terrible smell, and my father came up to me with a mirror and told me to look at myself. When I looked into the mirror I saw my mother's face. I screamed and woke up."

Irene says she doesn't know why this was so cathartic, but it turned out to be. "When I talked to my sponsor about the dream the next morning, I suddenly realized that my disgust with myself came from the disgust I felt—and the terror and responsibility—about taking care of my mother, cleaning up her body. It was such a terrible thing for a little girl to have to do! I had finally gotten to the core of my fear and shame. And as I began to relive those feelings, I started to cry, a different kind of crying than I'd ever done before. It wasn't the usual angry frustrated burst. It was full of *sadness*. That's what I hadn't allowed myself to feel: *sad*. I hadn't mourned what had happened to me as a little girl. I always knew I was supposed to forgive everybody, including my mother. I heard that in AA meetings all the time. But I had to get to this sadness before there was any possibility of feeling forgiveness. And my sponsor just hung on while I cried. She was completely silent for the long minutes it took me to discharge all of those tears. When I got my breath back and calmed down, she came up with a suggestion. 'I want you to take a bubble bath,' she said."

Irene said that she felt disappointed. "It sounded so self-helpy. Like one of those awful woman's magazine articles on how to deal with being stressed out. 'Do something nice for yourself! Buy yourself a present!' That sort of thing had always made me want to gag. But I was so depleted by now, so needy for any kind of guidance, my resistance so weak, that I took her suggestion." That night after the family was in bed, Irene got out a bottle of bubble bath her oldest son had given her the previous Mother's Day. She filled the tub with hot water and poured in the soap. She felt, she says, "a strange moment of panic. This was absurd! I needed to get to sleep. I had a long day of chores coming up. This was so childish, thinking a bubble bath would help anything!" But by now the tub was full, and the bubbles had piled high. "It did sort of look inviting. I thought I'd go through with it." Irene says she remembers slipping off her robe and catching a glimpse in the bathroom mirror of herself naked. "I looked so bony, so vulnerable. I shivered, even though it wasn't cold, with all the steam in the bathroom. But it was like something in the center of me was freezing, freezing for lack of contact, for feeling so alone." She eased herself into the tub. "I closed my eyes once I was fully submerged. It was *heaven*. All the buzz in my head, all the nattering away and getting mad at myself for being foolish, all the harsh self-criticism that had been raging away in my head, it all quieted down. This was the first sheer *pleasure* I could ever remember feeling. It wasn't something that helped me to numb out, like alcohol had once done. It was a real *feeling*. It was palpable, this sense of pleasure. I had never allowed myself to feel good before; that was the revelation. I soaped myself, ran a sponge over my breasts and my belly and down to my thighs. It was exquisite, this feeling of caressing myself. Why had I never been able to do this for myself before? I realized I'd always thought of my body as this dirty sort of mechanism, something that had to be cleaned and maintained and forced to go through its chores robotically. I didn't realize it was something you could take pleasure in, something you could love having."

Irene's bubble bath was a turning point for her. "It now occurs to me that there may be the possibility of pleasure or joy or contentment at the center of everything we do. Maybe all of life doesn't have to be drudgery. Even when it *is* drudgery, maybe we don't have to stop being curious or interested in what's going on. I got such a different sense of myself from this bubble bath. I was full of things to tell my sponsor the next day. The world suddenly seemed more manageable, interesting, worth exploring. I didn't magically become some sort of sensual free spirit and start dragging my husband to bed to have sex. But I've managed to be more affectionate with him in gentle nonthreatening ways. I'll kiss him when he comes home from work. I don't feel the need to be so distant. Something has broken in me. And part of what's released is my fear of talking to him. These past few weeks I've been able to be quite amazingly open about my fears, my sexual fears, the lingering disgust I still sometimes feel about making love. I'm talking to him about it. Just hearing myself say that is hard for me to believe! Life isn't a horrendous chore you have to grit your teeth and bear. I have a feeling of choice I didn't have before. And now, when I think of my mother and the little girl I was who took care of her, I don't feel such revulsion. I'm starting to accept the pain both my mother and I felt, not judge it, or push it away, or feel so much shame about it."

Irene, Marilyn, Ben, and Beth all discovered that the way they view their bodies mirrors not only the way they view their inner selves but also all of life. Life was something you either had to put up with (the way Irene steeled herself, robotically, to put up with her own physicality), ignore (as Marilyn sought to ignore, first through drugs, then through New Age meditative checking out, her obesity and physical pain) or take desperate pains to change (the way Ben and Beth desperately drove themselves to mold their muscles into some impenetrable fortress of perfection). In each case, the overwhelming feeling is that you have no choice but to fight who you really are in order to survive. Self-acceptance isn't only undesirable, it's unthinkable, somehow life-threatening! When we stop drinking and drugging, the degree to which we're still fleeing our secrets and our shame, our feelings of inadequacy and imperfection, is something we can no longer ignore. We're like a trapped animal running in circles in a mirrored room: whenever we open our eyes, we can't help seeing ourselves. Now that we're not drunk or high anymore, we can't escape the fact that we're *here*. And this means accepting that our bodies are here too.

It turns out that being here, having a body, doesn't have to be torture. The amazing news each of us can come to is that we don't have to be stuck with seeing ourselves the way we used to. As persistent as the vestigial, harshly self-critical views we learned to hold about ourselves may be, they don't have to block us. We have the power to hold them up to the light. We have the resources, especially those of Twelve-Step programs, to drain them of their venom.

Allowing ourselves to do this becomes possible as we give ourselves emotional *permission* to feel the pain, anger, resentment, and deep sadness we've been holding off all of our lives in the fear that their power will overwhelm or destroy us. At the same time, we can give ourselves the permission to take *pleasure* in our lives and in our bodies. Each of the people in this book has feared pleasure, and each has come to realize how big a block that fear of pleasure is. "I used to think that if I allowed myself to enjoy anything, I wouldn't be able to stop doing it," Irene says. "It's like what I used to think about alcohol when I drank: more was always better. But since that bubble bath, that's not what's happened. I'm not plunging into hot tubs all day! It's loosened me to take pleasure in other things as well. And of course it wasn't just the bubble bath that did it. I had to explore the sadness and disgust and shame I felt about my mother, all those terrible feelings I'd hid for so long, to get to the point where I *could* enjoy a bubble bath. Taking a bath is symbolic, I guess. Getting those emotions out was cleansing, sort of like taking an inner bath. And now, for some reason, all of life seems a little lighter, more manageable. Now that my fear has let up a bit, I don't feel that old reflex to escape."

Irene says this is what happens "at the best of times. I'm still very much a recovering—emphasis on *i-n-g*—alcoholic. I still clench. I don't feel like kissing myself when I look in the mirror. And though I'm talking more openly about my sexual fears with my husband, no one is going to start writing romance novels about us. I'm still blocked in a lot of ways. But it seems like there's a way out now. For the first time, I feel like I'll be able to survive my memories and feelings. I can have a body. I don't have to run away anymore. I keep thinking, What, really, is there to run away *from*? Fear has always been the bogeyman, and it turns out to be a phantom. Some feeling closer to love is starting to take its place."

CHAPTER 6

Moths and Flames: Romantic Obsessions

A first love that still haunts you, overshadowing every relationship you've since had, or tried to have . . .

A boss, a neighbor's spouse, a co-worker or a stranger on the street you can't get out of your mind . . .

One person, then another, then another—each of whom you're sure is "the one," each of whom turns out to be a miserable disappointment . . .

There turns out to be little romance in romantic obsessions. Feeling stuck to someone with whom we're unable to forge a satisfying relationship is a misery common to many of us in recovery. We may have sought help, turning to any number of books and therapists that promise to teach us how to deal with "codependent" or otherwise "dysfunctional" relationships. And yet, so often, after all the books we've read and all the therapists we've paid, we still feel stuck in the same old ruts. Sometimes we're tyrannized by the memory of a first love or a dead or divorced partner. Sometimes obsessive relationships are too much a part of our daily lives. But whatever our different particulars may be, we seem to be battling a common dilemma, an assumption that lies at the heart of every romantic obsession: *somebody out there can save me.*

The desire to be saved is one with which all recovering alcoholics and drug addicts are intimately familiar. The reason is simple: we all turned to drugs and/or alcohol to be "saved." We clung to them like life rafts: what else could rescue us so efficiently from our feelings, from having to face who we really were? Trained by years of drinking and drugging, we developed a well-oiled reflex to reach for something to "make it all better." It doesn't take much of a leap to turn that something into someone. Now that we've denied ourselves the outlet of booze and drugs, the impulse is often to grab for a human alternative: a perfect romantic or sexual partner who'll take away our loneliness and our pain, keep our fears at bay.

We're not always aware of this quick-fix tendency. We sometimes perceive and attempt to satisfy our sexual desires in the same way we may feel hungry and want a good meal. Sex, at such times, can seem completely divorced from love or from anything else in our lives, like fuel that we can fill up on when we need to. But the hunger for sex is deceptive; it usually turns out to be quite different from a stomach growling to be fed. More often it is connected to the growling of the *soul* to be fed. Even people like Martin, who feels he's totally objectified sex and severed it from any kind of conventional affectionate sentiment, eventually seem to discover that the primal urge impelling them has to do with something more than a desire for the release of orgasm. The hunger is for a more profound completion, *something to fill the void.* We usually want much more than we're conscious of wanting.

Sadly, once we begin to discover this hidden urgency—once we start to see just how powerful and tenacious the urge to grab for sex or romance is—we often end up hating ourselves, labeling ourselves failures. My usual self-berating litany goes something like this: Surely my inability to stop obsessing about someone marks me as stubborn, stupid, or weak. If I was working my program properly, I wouldn't keep falling into the same trap, would I? I'd know that I have to take responsibility for my own life, be accountable! I'd understand that all I have to do is "turn it over" and trust in my Higher Power and put my energy into doing the next right thing. I shouldn't *have* any problems, now that I know this, now that I have access to all the program "tools."

So why do I? Why do so many of us feel miserably stuck in our relationships or the memory of them? Why are we still so fearful? So controlling? So despondent? Are we all simply miserable failures at recovery? Have we all simply flunked the Third Step?

From my conversations with a range of recovering men and women, I've encountered a number of moving and successful attempts to answer these questions. First of all, fueled by fear, "romantic obsessors" tend to create one of three general scenarios: the "Rescue Me" syndrome, the "Love Equals Harassment" situation, or the "Vicarious Thrills" setup. Chances are good that you will resonate to one or more of these scenarios, even if you've never thought of yourself as romantically obsessed, so let's take a close look at them now.

RESCUE ME!

Adele, thirty-three and living in a midsize New England city, says she is no stranger to beating herself up for being and feeling needy. "Not that it helps much. Just knowing I feel needy doesn't make me stop being needy. It doesn't make me stop hating myself." Married for the past six years to Joe, a building contractor, with two kids, a five-year-old girl and a three-year-old boy, Adele is in her seventh year of sobriety. "I thank God daily that I didn't get married or have kids when I was still drinking," Adele says. "But I do sometimes wonder, a lot lately, if I shouldn't have paid more attention to that thing they tell you in AA meetings, not to get into a relationship in the first year. I wasn't five months sober before I met Joe and said yes when he asked me to marry him." Joe had been working on the two-family house where Adele lived. "It sounds funny. Joe comes across as this big, competent, macho contractor, but I met him because he hit himself on the thumb with a hammer. Before the day he came howling to my door, I hadn't paid much attention to him or his co-workers. They were working on the back porch, replacing some rotten boards, and they usually were gone by the time I got home from work. I'm a legal secretary, and in those days I was so blitzed by the newness of sobriety that it took me three times as long to get anything done as it does now. I was so distracted in those early days! So I usually got home late, long after the contractors had gone. But on one Monday they were working late too, and I heard this agonized yell and suddenly there Joe was at my door, looking like a six-year-old boy about to burst into tears. He asked if he could run his hand under some cold water. I let him in and finally made him call a doctor. He'd banged his thumb up pretty bad. Then this *mother* side of me just came out. That first moment should have given me a clue: it was our relationship in a nutshell. Big macho man breaks down, becomes a big baby, and comes home crying to mama. That sounds cynical and kind of nasty. I don't really mean it to. But lately it's what I've been feeling. These resentments!"

Adele shakes her head wearily. "Anyway, how we got together. He called me up after the thumb incident, and we
went out. I was so hungry for . . . all the things you're hungry
for in those first days of sobriety, endless approval, endless attention, unconditional love, a voice that says over and over
that you're okay and you're lovable. Joe was saying and doing
those things when we started out. Within two months he
asked me to marry him, and I said yes. I thought I'd found
somebody to take care of me. Unfortunately, he thought,
given the mama act I can be so good at, that he'd found somebody to take care of *him*."

Adele says that she was never really physically attracted to
Joe. "I've got a very specific type of fantasy man in my head:
blond, blue-eyed, quiet, athletic, educated, in control. Joe
doesn't fit it at all. He's lower-middle-class Italian, loud, emotions on his sleeve, a bit paunchy." But he seemed so sweet
and understanding and strong, at least when he wasn't banging himself with a hammer, that Adele convinced herself
she'd found someone she could grow to love. "I had all the
conventional ideas about sex and romance and marriage. My
mother, who drank secretly, was a stickler for keeping up appearances and gave long moral lectures about the true nature
of men and women. Women just weren't interested in sex the
way men were. Sometimes you had to pretend to keep the
peace. Of course I've since realized that the toll of pretending
is probably what made my mother turn to alcohol. Pretending
can't help but make you feel resentment, and she had to find
some way of letting her steam out. And I suppose I drank for a
lot of the same reasons. Trying so hard to live up to some kind
of standard of normality. Secretly feeling like an alien from
another planet. Desperately keeping up appearances so no-

body would find out I was a different species from everyone else. It's a kind of deep loneliness I've lived with my whole life, a sense of being separate that nothing and nobody can really touch. I'm terrified of that aloneness. I know that drinking helped me block it out. And the moment I stopped drinking, I couldn't keep it down anymore. It's no wonder I jumped at the chance, however illusory and unsatisfying it's turned out to be, to fill the hole in me with marriage."

What's been bothering Adele recently has to do with Dan, her boss. "It's basically this: I'm hopelessly in love with him." Dan is a perfect example of "the blond, athletic god, the kind of man who I can't imagine would ever take a second look at me. A number of guys of this type—usually very successful, powerful CEO types who have a sense of humor—have come into the office over the years. The humor is important. Maybe because I experienced so little of it when I was growing up. My father was a grouch, and my mother had this awful prim act. So much energy was dammed up in all three of us, it's a wonder we didn't all turn into homicidal maniacs! It's certainly no wonder that my mother and I dealt with it by drinking. My father dealt with it by having affairs. I didn't know about them until after they divorced, when I was nineteen, and my mother told me he'd been cheating on her for years. So maybe that's some kind of unconscious model for me too. I've come so close to asking Dan if he'd like to go to bed with me! Really outrageous stuff."

Until she met Dan, Adele was able to consign her frequent romantic daydreams about other men to the category of impossible fantasy. "They were almost always clients who came in for legal help. I'm the receptionist as well as secretary, and everybody has to go through me to get to the lawyers. There've been times I've felt my stomach drop right out of me when a man who fits the right type walks in. In a funny way, they look the way I used to think Joe was *inside*: someone who could take care of your every want, someone who could second-guess your needs before you knew what they were, someone who could just be eternally *there* for you. I suppose psychologically it's me looking for the perfect daddy, and also the perfect lover. Because I fantasize sex would be something indescribably wonderful with these dream men. I've never had an orgasm with Joe. To be honest, I've never come to orgasm with any man. I had almost no sexual experience before I met Joe. Alcohol had shut me down so completely, made me so paranoid and terrified of getting close to anyone. So all I had were my fantasies of what it might be like with one of my big blond powerful CEO gods. But, maybe fortunately, I never got so much as a bat of an eyelash from any of my crushes who walked into the office. Not until Dan, anyway."

Dan became one of the firm's law partners about a year ago. "From the moment he walked into the office, I was a goner," Adele said. "But what was really unnerving is that he was so incredibly solicitous of me! It's like he could see inside me. When I was in the least bit of a bad mood or nervous state, he'd pick up on it. 'You all right?' he'd ask in the most gentle and caring way. He'd compliment me on how I looked, what I was wearing. And my life changed. I began to really care about how I looked, not that I haven't always been burdened by my mother's legacy of putting appearances before all else; I have. But I'd given up for so long on attempting to look sexually attractive. Suddenly I was unbuttoning the top button of my blouse, wearing sheer silk, shorter skirts. I have a far-from-perfect figure, but I began to find ways to show off what I've got. My legs are good; I can carry off a shorter skirt. I started to use more expensive perfume. I began living for every chance encounter Dan and I would have. Slowly, he became the only important person in my life! I'd do everything I had to do at home: take care of my kids, make meals, go through the motions of being a nice and dutiful wife and mother. But I lived to get back to work. At first, all I was aware of was how wonderful it was to be around a man like Dan and feel like he actually wanted and liked my attentions. But the frustration began to set in pretty quickly."

The frustration took one particularly distressing form. "I began to wince every time Joe touched me or made any sexual overture. It's funny. I didn't mind the actual act of intercourse with him. That was somehow something almost athletic, definite. Once we were doing it, it was tolerable. It had a very specific end: Joe coming to orgasm, me taking care of him so he'd go to sleep! It was *getting* to it that was the problem. His tentative, gentle touches, the foreplay, I suppose, made me want to crawl out of my skin. It was him expressing *affection* for me that was so unendurable! I'd get ticklish, I'd feel annoyed, his touch was too light or too rough or too something else. I shudder even now, remembering what it felt like every time he reached out to me. And, naturally enough, he got more and more hurt. In fact, one night, when I was in my usual defensive sexual mode—sort of pushing him away, brushing his hands off me—he just stopped, sat up in bed, turned on the light, and confronted me. 'What's wrong? What am I doing wrong?' I had no idea what to tell him. But somehow, seeing him there, his big eyes hurt and wide and pleading, I felt this incredible surge of anger! It was like when he came howling to my door with his hurt thumb. He just seemed like this big baby. I couldn't feel any sympathy for him! I'd long ago decided that his constant desire for sex was just his way of handling anxiety: that he didn't really love or want me, he just wanted some kind of release and then to be mothered. Sex was some great neurotic act for him, to lay claim to me, make me care for him, make me pay attention to him, soothe his pain. And I wasn't having any of it anymore. Who was soothing *my* pain? What would he think if he knew that when we actually did have intercourse all I could think of was Dan? The more he seemed to plead for sympathy, the more I hated him! And on this night I couldn't hold these feelings of hatred and resentment back. I told him I couldn't stand making love to him. When he touched me, it made me sick!"

Adele pauses for a moment, the expression in her eyes sad and distant. "It was my own cruelty that got to me, the sheer lashing cruelty. I was almost put under by guilt. How could I have said these things to Joe? He didn't abuse me. He loved me. He put up with my emotional swings. And if he sought some kind of reassurance or felt the desire to be taken care of by me, was that so awful? Didn't he have needs too? He actually started to cry. I'd always known about Joe's neediness, but he wasn't the kind of man who cried. In fact, the only time I'd ever seen him cry was when he saw our first child for the first time. But I had wounded him very deeply. He didn't say anything. That was probably the worst part. He turned out the light and lay back down in bed, his back to me. Right then, right at that moment, I think we felt like the two most alone people in the world. My impulse was to reach out and touch him, hold him, comfort him, apologize. But sometimes when you need to do that most, you just can't. Something stops you. I think most of the sorrow in the world comes from people not comforting each other when they need to most. Why do we hold back just at the moment we need to give? I lay there on my back in the silence, trying to block out the sound of Joe's labored attempts not to cry, and did a sort of quick searching and fearless moral inventory of myself. The emotional pain had become so great that it was requiring me to take a look at it, to get beyond my own guilt at having hurt Joe, my own shame at my fantasies about Dan, my unwillingness to accept and fully acknowledge my own needs and wants and find some larger picture or perspective about what was going on. And something, suddenly, came up for me very clearly. It was like a voice, and I can remember the exact words: '*How could you love anyone who loved you?*' It hit me with the force of thunder that I cultivated my contempt for Joe's love and need for me because my own self-hate was still so great. It's like that old Groucho Marx quote about not wanting to join any club that would let you in. The revelation was like thunder, and I started to cry. It felt like a sadness that I'd been holding off my whole life. But now it all came out, in a torrent. Finally, I found the courage and strength and desire to reach over to Joe and hug him. Hug him like I'd never hugged him before . . . "

Joe and Adele didn't talk any further that night; they seemed, Adele says, to realize that at that point they needed simply to hold each other, give each other some kind of basic physical reassurance that they weren't alone. "It was like his neediness and my neediness just met blindly. He wasn't after sex anymore. Instinctively, I knew that. He was after what I had never been able to fully acknowledge that we both deserved: someone to love and be loved by." The next morning it was time to talk. "We're not mind readers. The last words Joe had heard from me was that he disgusted me sexually. He couldn't know the deeper nature of my feelings, of what I was going through, the insights I'd had, feeling so separate and alone in that bed. I had to *tell* him, to put into words that my feelings were tied to something that in a sense had nothing to do with him. They were tied to how inadequate and hopeless and unlovable I still felt I was. And it's funny, but nowhere in that morning talk did I once think of Dan! Later, after Joe left for work, the kids were off to day care and school, and I had a moment to have a lone cup of coffee before taking off for work myself, I had another revelation. I just didn't feel so tied to Dan, at least for that moment. He didn't seem like some kind of cure-all god, the way I'd fantasized up until that moment. Somehow, just acknowledging my feelings, the true urgency of my need for love and my fear that I don't deserve it, just letting that out lessened the urgency. Joe didn't fill me with such revulsion either. Something had let up. There was just less fear. And more love."

In the days and weeks since that morning, Adele has found that her insight is deepening. "I understand in my gut that hating Joe for loving me and losing myself in fantasies about Dan come from thinking I'm not enough. The real problem here is self-hate. But because of the nature of self-hate, you don't want to look at it. Looking at your self-hate just increases it! At least that's what I used to feel. I was terrified to go too deep in a fourth Step. In fact, it was because my sponsor kept getting on my back about doing a fourth Step that I once just about dropped her. I felt she was too coercive. But really I was afraid. I didn't want to look too deeply at myself. I was convinced that the feelings I'd find would be too malignant and powerful to tolerate. I've spent my whole life running away from these feelings, so reflexively that I haven't a clue anymore (if I ever did!) just what I'm running away from. Alcohol was my first savior, then Joe and his offer to take care of me in marriage, then, when I got too close to feeling loved by him, losing myself in fantasies of unattainable men. I was always fleeing something, always running away from whatever mirror kept rising out of the ground and showing me to myself."

Adele now accepts that her ability to come to any kind of breakthrough about this—her ability to acknowledge her feelings and come at least to the *idea* of self-acceptance—is entirely the product of her sobriety. "All these days and months and years of going to meetings, listening to other people's pain and breakthroughs, slowly tugging out my own experience, gaining strength and hope in the company of other alcoholics, and, above all, *not drinking* for all that time—all of it has gotten me here. I can't avoid looking into the mirror because, whether I was aware of it or not, I've spent all these years constructing a mirror to look into! Isn't that what the Steps are about? Look at your own part in your life. See what your own complicity is in your relationships. Again and again we're encouraged not to blame anyone or anything outside ourselves. I guess my fear, and my assumption, was that meant the only one left to blame was me. That's what I was running away from. The feeling that I was *guilty* for everything, including the weather! But now, well, I guess the real breakthrough I've had is understanding that even *I'm* not to blame. It's not a question of blame! It's a question of *clarity*, of accountability. So much of my sobriety now seems geared to teasing out the cause and effect of things, to see how A leads to B leads to C, not to judge it. Just *look* at it and learn from it. When I see my own life and fears in this less charged way, I can let up on myself. And let up on my need to flee my own feelings. Which means I feel less of a compulsive urge to flee Joe and dream my day away about Dan and more of a willingness to live life without shutting down."

My conversations with recovering people vividly rein-
force the general psychological truth that we perceive all relationships symbolically. This includes the relationship we
developed between ourselves and drugs and alcohol, something Adele has become especially aware of. She now sees
that she turned to alcohol as a kind of best friend, something
to take her out of herself, away from any feeling that even re-
motely threatened her. In sobriety, she saw Joe symbolically
as a another kind of savior, offering a marriage that she
hoped would take care of her, a marriage that would be a
stand-in for a perfect, unconditionally loving parent. Later,
after she'd experienced Joe's love, the symbol he represented
changed. Now he was something to be despised. Deeply, as
much as she yearned for love, she was almost constitutionally incapable of accepting it when it was offered. Because
she'd never loved herself, and thus was never able to experience any kind of self-acceptance, she couldn't conceive of
anyone else accepting or loving her. Other people's love
amounted to some kind of neurotic neediness. So she fled again,
this time to a new symbol, a new savior to rescue her: the knight
in shining armor, Dan. He was distant enough not to really
threaten her. She could keep the idea of him loving her a fantasy. She wouldn't have to go through the actual *experience* of it,
an experience she couldn't conceive of allowing herself.

This dynamic of fear, self-hate, and escape is very common
to people in recovery. But as clear as the solution may appear
to be—learn to let up on yourself, stop judging, move toward
more self-acceptance and self-love—it's by no means easy to
effect it. It seems to take the kind of slow, patient accruing of
sobriety that Adele talks about experiencing. "You never
know what insights are growing inside you," she says. "The
only thing I'm sure of, from my own experience, is that some

kind of self-acceptance and self-love seem to be inevitable as long as I keep nurturing my recovery."

WHEN LOVE EQUALS HARASSMENT

As symbolic as relationships are, they are also more than that. We need to learn that we are more than pawns on a chessboard, more than archetypes battling each other in some inescapable unconscious myth. Looking at the symbolic ways we view sexual and romantic partners can give us a lot of data about ourselves; we can benefit enormously by teasing out the meaning of those symbols. But we also need to remind ourselves that we're *people*, not the larger-(and simpler)-than-life gods, demons, or cartoon cutouts we sometimes make each other into. We're capable of an enormous range of responses, feelings, behaviors. As we begin to accept that we're more than we thought we were, we need to accept that the people around us are more faceted and less categorizable than we once allowed ourselves to see. We can't pigeonhole anyone for long. We discover that nobody fits any simple niche.

This lesson is a hard and sometimes frightening one. Sometimes we have to go through hell to learn it.

At forty-four, Rick felt, until very recently, like a very large part of him was still twenty-four. "That was when my first lover dumped me," he says. "It's taken me twenty years to get over it." Rick says he finds this "deeply embarrassing. I've been in recovery for five years now. I've grown and changed in so many ways. I really messed up my life, got into incredible debt, was thrown in jail for drunk driving, disorderly conduct, stealing. I lost everything: friends, family, home, job, money. And I've clawed my way back. Well, sometimes it feels like clawing, although that sounds like I did it all myself.

Recovery teaches me I don't do anything by myself, and it's made me glad that that's true. There's always abundant help to be had. But in this one area—the geography of my soul I've labeled in big bold letters J I M—I was as stuck at forty-four as I ever was at twenty-four."

Rick met Jim in the small campus town of the college they both had gone to in rural Pennsylvania. "It was one of those expensive, elitist, highly selective schools," Rick says. "I got a lot of feeling of prestige from going there. Not that I did all that well. But I managed to graduate from it—no mean feat, given the amount I was beginning to drink and the drugs I was taking. It was like my one badge of respectability and honor: I had a degree from this hot-shit school. Unfortunately, I didn't have a clue what to do next. All my respectable energies had gone into graduating college. When I got out, I was completely at sea. Didn't know where else to live but in the town I'd spent my last four years in. Couldn't imagine moving to some city. I had no money, and I didn't have enough self-confidence to think I could make any. I was terrified, really. So I stayed where I was. Found a clerk job in a music store downtown."

Rick met Jim in the store. "Jim was the manager. It's funny. I remember not liking him very much when I first met him. I picked up on only two things, neither of them very enticing. One was that Jim had this incredibly deep, loud speaking voice. The other was that he was moody as hell, sullen. Walked around in this dark cloud most of the time." But even when Rick hadn't liked Jim much, he still felt a kind of obligation to him, a strong urge to do everything right so Jim would think highly of him. "It was more than that Jim was the boss. There was something about him that made me want to do my job perfectly. I wanted to *please* him. Even before I fell in love with him, I wanted to do whatever he asked me to, perfectly, so he couldn't find fault with me."

In his junior year, Rick had spent some time in Paris, a half year abroad during which time he "discovered" he was gay. "Well, that's not really true. I always knew I was attracted to men, but in Paris I allowed myself to act on it. It was such a strange dose of sophistication in the middle of my college career: to Paris from Podunk, Pennsylvania. When I came back to college, I almost dropped out. I'd had a slight taste of it being all right to be gay. This was in 1969, just when things were beginning to open up sexually, even though in Paris at that time people were still pretty closeted and stereotypically limp-wristed about it. But the point was, I found out there was a *world* out there. Coming back to small-town Pennsylvania was a devastating shock. That's when I started drinking and smoking pot heavy duty." By the time he met Jim, Rick had all but given up on meeting anyone gay in college. "Actually, on the sly in the deserted locker room of the school swimming pool, I did meet a couple faculty members, older men who nervously came on to me. And there was this or that episode of furtive, guilty sex in the men's room of the library. Stuff like that. But nobody I could imagine ever having a relationship with." Nothing about Jim signaled that he was gay, so Rick had no expectations of a romantic relationship at first.

"Things began to change when Jim discovered I loved Mozart as much as he did. Jim had graduated from the college four years before me, so we never knew each other as students. He was probably as lost as I was, but to me, as I got to know him, he seemed like this incredibly independent man who'd turned his back on the world and decided to live a simple life in the country. I didn't realize then that Jim was as afraid as I was to leave that town. All his bluster and definite opinions—

and, boy, were his opinions definite!—meant to me was that he'd made a wise, conscious choice to live like a sort of small-town Thoreau. He was a brilliant guy. He had an encyclopedic knowledge of opera, especially Mozart's operas. I'm a pretty good pianist, and when Jim found that out, he had me come over to his house and listen to Walter Gieseking playing Mozart sonatas, real old recordings. I just took it on faith that Jim had the right opinions about everything, Mozart performance included. He was just so sure about everything. A pattern was quickly set: he was the teacher, I was the student. And he certainly did know more than I did. His enthusiasm was genuine. He adored Mozart, thought he was God, and I saw him come to tears more than once as he took me by the hand through *Figaro* and *Cosi Fan Tutte* and *The Magic Flute*."

At first, Rick says, "by the hand" was just metaphorical. But, one night, it turned into more than that. "We'd get together with a bottle of Cutty Sark and the libretto of whatever opera we were going to dissect that night and sit on the couch next to each other. He loved to drink as much as I did. So we'd just sit there on the couch, getting more and more plowed and more and more weepy as Beverly Sills or Mirella Freni or whoever it was trilled her heart out. This one night, overcome with emotion, Jim flopped back on the couch and lay his head in my lap. There were no words. That was just it. He just lay there, with tears in his eyes, lying on my lap. I was petrified. Nothing had passed between us to indicate that either one of us was open to physical intimacy. Which means we didn't know the other was gay. I just sat there in a state of panic and excitement, completely motionless, my heart beating like a hammer, and felt the weight of his head and shoulders on my legs. I was drunk, but maybe he was drunker. He reached up his hand and, with his eyes closed, started to touch my hair, blindly groping for it. It was so romantic, and touching, like a child reaching out fearfully for affection, reassurance. I reached for his hand and brought it to my lips, kissed it. He groaned like he was in pain, extracted himself from me, dragged himself off the couch, and went over to the lamp by the side of the stereo to turn it off. Then, in the dark, he walked back to me."

This began the first of several sexual encounters that Rick says were always completely wordless. "We never talked about what we were doing, not the first few times. In fact, sometimes, a day after we'd made love—and the pattern was always the same: scotch, Mozart, tears at how beautiful it all was, and then silent dark groping—I was almost convinced it wasn't happening. Jim was just as blunt and officious and loud and rude to me at work the next day as he'd ever been before. The few times he did talk to me about his life and his past relationships, all he talked about were his love affairs with women. Sometimes I thought I was going crazy. Like what we did with each other at night wasn't even happening!"

The signal moment Rick hasn't been able to get out of his mind happened about three months into the affair. "Jim was taking care of this really nice house for an elderly couple who were away on vacation. It was winter, real snowy. He asked me to come over and listen to music. It was an incredible house, eighteenth-century, with one of those big stone fireplaces you could just about walk into. Jim had made a big fire; it was all the light there was in the house. He put on his favorite recording of *Idomeneo*. But this time he didn't wait for us to get drunk so we could go through with having sex. He just walked over to me—we both were standing—and he looked into my eyes. He didn't say anything; he just looked into my eyes. He started to unbutton my shirt. He slipped it off me. Then he undid my pants, helped me step out of them. I stood in front of him, in the firelight, naked. He didn't touch me. He just looked at me. I'm not sure, but I think he was crying a little. It was hard to tell in the light. Then he said, real quiet, that he thought I was the most beautiful person he'd ever seen. And that he wished he could marry me."

They made love that night in a real bed, not sprawled drunk over a couch as they usually did. Rick remembers it being wonderful, but the details have blurred. What hasn't blurred at all is the memory of standing in front of Jim in the firelight. "That's the image that haunts me, makes me nuts. After all that's happened, that's the image I keep going back to. I can't get it out of my mind. It's the only time in my life I felt truly adored, truly loved. It's like I've set that scene in amber. It will never change, never go away. Like something on Keats's Grecian urn."

Rick sums up the rest of his relationship with Jim neatly. "It was all downhill from there. Lots of things went wrong. Partly, I think, it was Jim's fear of having been so emotionally open. He started, almost the day after that, to find more fault than usual in everything I did. He got very depressed. I knew even then that it had nothing to do with me. It's like some terrible black cloud would descend, a cloud Jim had no power to avoid, and he'd be stuck in it for hours, sometimes days at a time. He'd do nothing but grunt at me then. Carp at everything. I remember once I came over in the morning and offered to cook breakfast, and he said, 'Sure, go ahead,' and then he stood in the kitchen while I cooked bacon and eggs. Everything took too long for him. He criticized me for every move I made. I almost threw the pan at him. I started to hate him. Gradually, it got so the only way we knew how to relate to each other was to lash out or withdraw. He hated anything

I loved, except for Mozart, and even that he felt he had the superior response to. I used to like Joni Mitchell; Joni Mitchell
made him sick. I liked the wrong flavor ice cream. If I'd been
the sort of superior being he was, I would have had his tastes.
That's the message I kept getting."

And yet, Rick says, he was "hooked. As unhappy as I was,
my world revolved around Jim. We had some of the most te-
dious, drawn-out, hateful evenings brooding in the dark I
could possibly imagine, and yet I couldn't imagine ever separating from him. It was like some dark chain locked me to
him. Whenever things would get bad, and that's all they were
by the end of that first year, I'd still somehow go back in my
mind to that firelit winter evening when he told me he loved
me. I'd cling to that, as if that were the only true reality . . . "

Eventually, Jim made a momentous decision. "He was going
to graduate school far away, at the University of Chicago.
They'd offered him a fellowship, a teaching assistant deal with
full paid tuition. Jim was one smart man, I tell you. He decided
he had to get away and take it. I was devastated. I couldn't
imagine how I was going to live without him. But in two
months, he was gone." Rick shudders at the memory of what
the next months and years were for him. "I really started
drinking like a madman. I remember one snowy evening dragging every book, every stick of furniture, every record, every
sweater, every pot and pan Jim had left with me when he went
to Chicago out the door and throwing it all in the bushes,
which were covered with snow. I'd call him and then slam the
phone down. Or send telegrams with scathing messages. I
hounded him like a totally insane person. Once I actually took
a bus all the way to Chicago and stood outside his building
waiting for him to come out. When he did, I trailed him down
the street to see where he was going. I was incredibly jealous. I

wanted to see who his new lover was. I wanted to . . . well, I wanted to kill him. Or get back at him. Yeah, that was it. I wanted vengeance. I wanted him to see how hurt I was . . . "

For his part, Jim cut off all communications with Rick after a final letter that read in toto (and in capital letters): LEAVE ME ALONE.

The saga of Rick's next fifteen years is one he tells when he speaks at AA or NA meetings. "My life quickly turned to shit. I finally moved to Philadelphia and lived in a rat trap, a cheap and unspeakably filthy single room. I'd forget about Jim for a while, get into one or another sexual relationship, cheat on whoever it was, go to the baths. When I was young and good-looking enough, sometimes I'd hustle, sell my body for that week's rent. God, the endless sex I had! But even when I forgot about Jim, the quality of everything I did felt like vengeance. It was like the unspoken motive was 'Take *that!*' Some part of the messed-up, addicted, alcoholic me was convinced that every hurtful thing I did to myself was in fact hurting Jim. I was in a constant state of revenge. The years went by. Sometimes, full of fear and alcohol, I'd try to get in touch with Jim. I remember getting plowed one night, it was Jim's birthday, and I called him up—I kept finding his number and address through the college almuni records—and I blubbered on. He hung up on me. My life just kept spiraling down. I was thrown out of the room I lived in at one point. It was late fall. I remember walking the streets, wondering if I could drum up the courage to kill myself. I stole a pint of wine out of the hands of a nearly comatose bum somewhere in South Philly and drank myself into oblivion. My last memory was the look in Jim's damned eyes as he told me, for the eighty-millionth time, that he loved me."

Rick woke up and realized that he'd gotten as low as he could without actually being dead. "It turned out, although I didn't know it then, to be my spiritual awakening. I went to the Salvation Army for coffee and a roll. An AA meeting was going on in the next room. There was more coffee there, so I went in. And I listened. And I knew, in that instant, that I was home."

That was a little over five years ago. "Like I said at first, my life has gotten unbelievably better. So much has lifted from me, so much self-hate. I've got a wonderful job now teaching English and music at a great prep school. The kids love me. I have a tiny apartment I've lavished with care; it's really beautiful. When I compare my life now with the hell I went through for all those years, I'm filled with so much gratitude I could cry. But something else made me cry too, in a different way. It was that damned memory of Jim. It just wouldn't go away. With all the wonderful things that have happened to me in sobriety, I was still as stuck as I ever was with that taunting memory, the memory of the only magical feeling of love I've ever felt in my life. I kept badgering myself: When would it go away?"

One way Rick tried to escape the feelings his memories keep bringing up was to look for sex. "To tell you the truth, I don't feel capable of falling in love anymore. I guess I was so fixated for so long on Jim that it drained that capacity out of me. I can't help but think 'falling in love' is just some kind of neurotic self-delusion. You're always projecting some imagined perfect partner onto an unwilling and very imperfect human being. Falling in love can't help but lead to disaster. Doesn't my own experience tell me that? I mean, even I know that I was miserable with Jim. The thing I'm holding on to is really the memory of *one night*. The rest was really terrible. We disliked each other intensely most of the time. Apart from Mozart, we had very little in common. I can get very cynical about all this: frustrated, because I can't give up that one romantic memory, but cynical. And when I get cynical, I grab out for a quick fix: an anonymous body to have sex with."

Rick has been relatively careful in this age of AIDS: "I don't do anything unsafe. Physically, anyway. But emotionally . . . " In sobriety, Rick has found most of his partners through answering personal ads by letter or meeting men on the phone. "They have these special numbers you can call where you just get this disembodied voice with whom you try to establish, within seconds, whether or not there's sexual chemistry. Mostly you get a grunted, 'Hey. What're ya into? What d'ya look like?' And usually, when you tell him, an abrupt click signals that you're not what whoever the grunt was looking for, and you're on to the next grunt. But sometimes you connect." Most of Rick's sexual liaisons have been disappointing, however. "Few people look like they say they do." He went through all the available phone lines listed in local gay newspapers and had very little luck with any of them. "Then, well, it's not that my luck in meeting anybody changed, but something did change my attitude about it all."

Rick discovered a phone line that was essentially a list of recorded come-ons by dozens of men. "It was a line you paid to leave a message and your phone number on. You only had twenty seconds to say what you were into. Twenty seconds to turn on a prospect, tell him everything you wanted him to know about you, sell yourself, give your deepest and most intimate fantasy. Twenty seconds, really, to lasso whoever might be drifting by. I started listening to the messages. My head spun. They went something like: 'Hey, dude, I'm thirty-five, five-ten, 175, smooth body, looking for a Sting-look-alike . . . '

'I'm twenty-eight, 275, looking for a chubby chaser to love me for the rest of my life . . . ' 'Sixty, not very attractive, very imaginative in bed, lonely . . . ' 'Nineteen, straight-appearing, please be very discreet when you call . . . ' 'Have this wrestling fantasy . . . ' 'No fats or fems . . . ' 'only Oriental . . . ' 'black . . . ' 'Irish . . . ' 'Want to walk on the beach . . . ' ' . . . the woods . . . ' ' . . . travel . . . ' 'lonely . . . ' 'hot . . . ' 'new to this . . . ' 'willing . . . ' "

Rick says he was dumbfounded. "You know, one of the central and most healing things about AA and NA is that before long you learn that you're not alone. It's maybe the single most important thing I've learned in program. I'm not alone. Other people have had feelings like mine. Other people understand." Rick sighs. "But this litany of people baring their fantasies, baring their need for someone, trying so desperately to connect . . . I just found it so incredibly moving. Because I was reminded, once again, how fragile we all are. How desperate we all are for love. And I could feel in this moment more compassion for my own neediness. I have never truly believed it was okay to express this neediness. It's like some terrible weakness that people like Jim can't help but hate me for. But now I can see that the only problem is my own *desperation*. My own deeply entrenched belief that I was the only one who felt this degree of need. In the space of ten minutes of listening to this recorded list of desperate voices, I clued into the hungers of thirty different men, men who were shouting, whispering, posturing, cajoling, bragging, pleading into the void: 'Somebody out there, love me.' Even the most out-and-out sexual come-on, the most lust-ridden proposition seemed like just one more cry for attention, love, help. Maybe I'm overreacting. Maybe not everyone was as desperate as all that. But the point is, I was able to make contact with my *own* hunger for love. And for some reason, I see how I've treated myself and Jim in a whole new way."

The first dividend has been the most surprising. "Finally, twenty years later, I've truly been able to let go of Jim. I really don't feel fixated on his memory in the same old way. I wish I could explain exactly how and why this has happened. The closest I can come is to say that as I've given myself permission to acknowledge my own desire for love, it's freed me to accept myself more, to join the human race. All those voices on the tape and all the voices I hear in AA and NA teach me that I'm not so different from anyone else. We're all stumbling around, trying to do our best. Jim is stumbling around too, doing his own best. I can let him alone and wish him well. I don't have to cling to him like a barnacle. I don't need to hound him anymore, because I've discovered I don't need to keep hounding and hating myself. He's free from me now because I'm free from myself, free from at least the worst of those old clutching desperate fears. I don't need to act them out on anyone else, which is exactly what I now realize I was doing to Jim."

We are all perhaps unavoidably self-referential: we can't quite believe in something until it happens to *us*. You don't know what recovery is until you yourself start to recover. The same thing seems to apply to compassion: self-compassion almost automatically allows you to feel more empathy for and understanding of other people. There's a kind of inescapable domino effect as we begin to care for ourselves, an effect that seems to color our perceptions of the rest of the world. Rick was finally able to get over his obsession with Jim when he allowed himself to accept the fear underlying it. His desire for love was so urgent because he deeply feared never having it met by anyone but Jim. He fixed on that firelit moment so many years before because it was the only moment of his life he had ever felt his desire for love being met. Psychically, he felt he had to somehow get that moment *back*: Wasn't it his only chance to experience love again? But in sobriety, through a growing willingness to imagine and empathize with other people and to accept his own wants and needs, Rick is beginning to feel more emotional spaciousness and to give *himself* the love he seeks. He now sees that there might be other sources of love than the one he long ago feared was his only hope. He can let the fire in his memory burn gently to ashes. Jim doesn't have to be any longer Rick's only hope of love. Love is available from many, many other sources, something he hadn't dared, until now, to believe could be true.

VICARIOUS THRILLS

The decision that "there's only one way you can get love" from which Rick is starting to free himself has led Teri into some very distressing scenarios, what she calls "serial catastrophes."

"My pattern was pretty clear to me even when I drank and did drugs," says Teri, who at twenty-eight has just over three years of sobriety in AA. "It's always seemed like some ironic twist of fate that I kept ending up with the men I did. I mean, I was such a goody-two-shoes for most of my life. Wanted to save the world. Became a nurse, got a responsible job in a good hospital. This was back in the days when I was able to confine my drinking to late nights and weekends, so I was still able to function. But I came home to some unbelievable creeps. Here I was, working my rear off, and the men I got involved with were invariably unemployed, emotionally disturbed, artsy types, failed poets and the like. They all had grandiose visions of the world discovering them; that was one thing that united them. Jerry wore the same torn T-shirt for weeks on end. He reeked, which when I was in the mood I found sexually exciting; when I wasn't, it nauseated me. He smoked pot nonstop. I'd come home to clouds of the stuff, like I was in some opium den. His motto was 'Screw it.' He wrote stream-of-consciousness poetry on my typewriter, which he regularly broke. He was such a sensitive artist, he said, that when he got angry he had no choice but to bust things up. Wouldn't I rather he bust up my typewriter than me? Finally, I had to get an order of protection to keep him out of the apartment. Eventually even I had enough of him. Then there was Mark. Now there was a prize. Mark introduced me to the joys of heroin. I was the only nurse I knew who mainlined every Saturday night. He also invited all of his friends over at all hours, down-and-out types I'd find at various times of night and day nodding out into the refrigerator, draped over the bathtub, or huddled on the bedroom floor. 'Life is a party,' Mark kept saying. If it was, only the living dead had been invited. By the end, I had to change the locks on my apartment to keep him out. There were others. Motorcycle guys, drunks, rebels without causes, lost souls. I somehow kept this incredible respectable front up at work. God knows how I continued to function, but I did. It was like I had this whole seamy smoky world at home nobody knew about. Sure, there was obviously something very exciting about it to me. I know now that there had to be a payoff for me to keep getting hooked to the same kind of men over and over. But I wasn't really able to see what my own complicity in all this was until after I got sober, which I did after ending up in a hospital after a near fatal overdose of heroin. Thank heavens it wasn't the hospital I worked at. Discovering how and why I've engineered my life this way has been the most uncomfortable thing I've had to do in sobriety."

Teri's sponsor helped her explore own motivations more deeply. Her sponsor was "a woman, Anna, whom I chose for some of the same reasons I'd chosen the loser men I kept getting involved with. That doesn't sound very nice, implying Anna was a loser! But in a way, that's what I thought. I was so intimidated by all those clean, 'happy, joyous, and free' people I often saw in AA and NA. Not that there weren't people like me, people who were suspicious of being fed a line, suspicious of what often sounded like Romper Room jargon. There were. And Anna was very definitely one of them. In fact, it was the sense I got that Anna wasn't buying the whole ball of wax that made me think there was some possibility of relating to her. What I've found, though, is that appearances can be very deceiving. I used to pride myself on being able to size up personalities at first glance. Thankfully, it turns out, I was very wrong about sizing up Anna."

Anna appeared to be, in Teri's terse description, "a mess. Nothing she wore matched. Her hair stuck out at strange angles. Partly it was a sort of punk look, but only by default. She never seemed to have the time to pay attention to her looks, or much of anything else. Life always seemed to be bolloxing her up. She was forgetful, always late, had a hard time juggling priorities. But she had a kind of free spirit I found awfully appealing. As chaotic as her appearance and life seemed to be, she was incredibly *funny*. She has the best sense of humor, this delicious sense of the absurd, of anyone I've met. Maybe the thing that attracted me the most was her stance, which I found so hard to believe myself, that things just weren't so damned *serious*. Life was a kind of circus: no rules, anything went, as long as you didn't really screw up the works by drinking and drugging. As maddening as she could sometimes be,

Anna was and is very strong on that one point. Don't go out of the way to kill yourself. We'll all die soon enough . . ."

Anna has helped Teri with something central. "The very first time we met, after I asked her to be my sponsor and she consulted her completely chaotic calendar and said, 'Sure, why the hell not?' Anna gave me her take on me. I thought I was good at sizing people up? Anna was so on the mark about me it left me breathless. I hadn't even told her about the long string of loser men in my life. But she said, right off, she suspected that every person I got involved with was doing something I wished I could do myself. I was anal retentive and secretly ached to say 'Screw it!' to the world and relax and just do anything I wanted to without thinking or caring. But I couldn't do that. I was made of guilt. So I hooked up with people who could. I lived through them. Sure, I hated it after a while. It kicked up every resentment in me. How could they get away with being so heedless, so uncaring? The very qualities I was attracted to turned into reasons for loathing them. I despised the people I started out loving because they were getting away with something I couldn't possibly allow myself. The drinking, the heroin, all of that helped a little to get the rod out of my you-know-what. But I was born with that rod; it was as much a part of me as my spine. I couldn't change. I would always be rigid and guilty. But I felt so trapped that I still felt the impulse to find people who didn't care about anything. I kept hoping, somehow, that attitude would rub off . . ."

Teri reiterates that Anna was completely right. "I could see something else too. After a time, I always wanted to fix the men in my life, make them 'behave' the way I thought they should, which is to say the way I was brought up to think I had to. After a sort of honeymoon period of allowing them to lie around and screw off, I'd start to come up with projects, voice harsh opinions of what they ought to be doing with their lives. It was true what Anna said, that I ended up resenting the very things that attracted me. It was an incredibly confining, stifling rut."

Teri is beginning to talk about, and sometimes very tentatively accept, the possibility that she may not have to go outside herself for the feeling of "wild" freedom she yearns for. Deeply hidden as it is, she has her *own* wild, abandoned, joyous self, one she might be able to summon up and even enjoy without resorting to anyone or anything external to her. But this is a very new feeling and completely opposite to most of the messages she's given herself throughout her life. "I realize now that the only time I really could let loose with my no-good bums was either when we were drunk or on drugs or having sex. Of course, all three usually came together. But the greatest sexual intensity was me feeling I'd trapped one of these wild animals in bed. It was a feeling of conquest and secrecy, like some African trapper poaching some endangered species. Maybe if I could *fuck* one of these creatures completely enough, sort of squeeze some kind of precious magical elixir out of them along with their sperm, I'd somehow take in whatever wildness they were made of, make it part of *me*. But I kept waking up the same hung-over, guilt-ridden woman. And there they were, damn them, one after another, comatose and completely oblivious and *untouched*. I couldn't, finally, wrench out of them whatever it was I so desperately needed. That *freedom* of self, the ability to just let 'er rip. I couldn't get it out of them, not really. And so I resented the hell out of every one of them. If those no-good bums couldn't turn me into a no-good bum, what use were they?"

The new idea that the freedom Teri is seeking has to come from within her has turned out to be the most intriguing discovery she's made. "I've always accepted on some kind of head level that you can't get an identity from other people. In fact, I'm very sensitive to people whining and going on and on about how badly the world has treated them. I grew up with this rigid, pull-yourself-up-by-your-own-bootstraps mentality. You don't have something? Don't complain about it, go out and get it! I'm the harshest judge of other people in this way, and obviously I put myself through the wringer too. But now, after Anna's diagnosis of me, for some reason I'm seeing that that's exactly what I've tried to do my whole life: extract some essence, some real sense of self from other people. I was the most severely *dependent* person imaginable! Anna tells me this doesn't have to turn into one more reason to hate myself. She says, of course I want a sense of freedom, a comfortable, free sense of who I am. Of course I hunger for that. There's every reason in the world why I should try to cultivate that, gain a wider and more permissive sense of options in my life, find that freedom. But I should realize that it has to come from within. That's the only secret about it. You can't get it from outside yourself. It's something you've got to give yourself. And not without help either. I'm finding, slowly, that I can transfer my dependent feelings to AA, to other people who aren't out to exploit me, to people who are wrestling with the same fears and demons I am. I can depend on them for sympathy and guidance and love. It's okay, in fact, to be as dependent as I want to be. Because that dependence is in service of helping me to develop a real, rooted sense of comfort. I wouldn't keep working away at my sobriety now if I didn't hope it would give me that. With Anna's and everybody else's help, that hope is turning into certainty. I don't need a bum to abuse me to give me some second-hand feeling of freedom. There are so many more loving and productive ways to acquire it."

Romantic obsessions challenge us in some unanticipated ways. We've seen everyone in this chapter move from perceiving their sexual and affectional fixations as threats, burdens, or afflictions to seeing them as keys to something basic about who they are and what they really want. Our romantic blocks can turn out to be opportunities to examine how we view ourselves and the world and how those views might be holding us back, preventing us from the freedom and sense of self we so desperately crave. But we shouldn't run from, shun, or judge this hunger for freedom and identity, for contact, love, connection, affection to fill the void. We don't need new ways to ignore or stamp out that hunger. *We need to find ways to truly satisfy it.* We all know from painful experience that drinking and drugs can't satisfy it. We're also learning, by the example of our own lives as well as those of the people in this book, that turning to romance and sex as cure-alls is just as unproductive. A sense grows in us that the answer lies in giving ourselves a deeper kind of permission, the permission to go as far into our hungers as we can, not to lop them off prematurely as we do when we flee compulsively to one escape hatch or another, whether it's booze, drugs, food, money, or sex. The answer lies in us developing the willingness to *experience* feelings so that we can learn truly what we want. Recovering people who make love consciously are people who take joy in pleasure, in satisfying their desires. They're people who give themselves permission to be themselves.

All the people in this book have moved toward giving themselves this permission. Now come some deeper sighs of relief.

CHAPTER 7

How to Make Love
While Conscious

"People are a pain in the neck," Pauline an-nounces cheerfully. "That's my big revelation for this year." This revelation, Pauline says, is the product of the past twenty-three months, during which time she met Chris, fell in love with him, fell into panic at the idea of falling in love with Chris, hated Chris, learned to love him again, and now has decided to marry him. "Chris went through a similar roller coaster ride, although his swings up and down and back and forth didn't always coin-cide with mine. Which is part of the point."

Pauline says that perhaps the most baffling and disturbing thing about all of her ups and downs is that she felt she wasn't supposed to have them. There wasn't a moment when she and Chris weren't assiduously working their respective programs in AA. Shouldn't that have prevented anything negative from happening? "We've both been sober for about six years," she says, "and when we met, we really felt we were as ready as any two sober people could be. We'd both been wary about getting involved with anyone in the first two years of sobriety, kept very close to sponsors, went to meetings virtually every day, and were very careful to take things slow when we met and started dating. I don't mean we thought of ourselves as model recoverers, exactly. We both struggle with fear and resentment and low self-esteem, just like most other people in recovery. But we really were taking things by the Big Book—turning it over, talking it over, praying for guidance, applying Twelve-Step principles as consciously as we could. I think both of us thought that after all the pain and despair and confusion we'd each been through, *now*, finally, we could relax. We're good, caring, loving, sober people. And we're attracted to each other! What could be better? What could go wrong?"

Actually, Pauline says, nothing *did* go wrong in the first days, weeks, and months of going out with Chris. "It was heaven. Chris was so different from the men I'd been involved with before. He was so reliable, for one thing. He has a good job in a big insurance company, his friends seemed to be easy-going, stable types, which was a whole new trip for me. I've always been pretty ambitious and hardworking, as far as that goes. I've got a good job in the P.R. department of a major chain of department stores—been promoted twice in the past three years. But I always got myself hooked to these under-achievers, people whose outward lives reflected how I felt about myself inside. Until recently, I always felt like an impostor. I can put on this wonderfully competent, officious managerial act, but the real me is a fake. I'd always felt on the verge of going out of control, being found incompetent. I know I'm not alone in this. It's helped to hear so many other recovering people talk about their own discomfort with success; it's a real problem for us in recovery. But I felt I'd made a few strides by the time Chris and I met. And, as I got to know him better, I got the sense that he felt he'd made strides too. I think we were both delighted at the prospect of becoming normal human beings after so many years of hiding, drinking, feeling miserable, and surrounding ourselves with losers. We had a shot at something we never thought we could have when we were out there drinking or even in the first three or four years of our sobriety. We could have *lives*."

This spirit of optimism made their first dates wonderfully satisfying. "Both of us had a history of falling into bed on first dates when we drank. But now it was like we were back in high school. I remember the first time he kissed me good-night and left me at my door, I felt seventeen again! Well, more like fourteen. By seventeen I was already drinking cases of Colt 45 and smoking pot. But Chris brought me back to a feeling of innocence. I had the sense with him that we could really start over. We took things very slowly."

Pauline says Chris was as happy during these early days as she. "We were just so *proud* of each other. Kept introducing each other to our friends with a kind of 'Look who I found! Aren't I lucky?' attitude. We adored each other. Everything between us felt so healthy. We'd hike and swim and do outdoor things I'd never done before. Chris is more adventurous than any other man I'd known, and he's gotten me to be too. We actually went sky diving once! Sometimes I saw my time with him as if it were a movie happening to someone else: Who was this incredibly fortunate woman? After years of not being able to imagine hooking up with a man I could truly love, a man I might even want to marry, suddenly I had someone who embodied all I could wish for."

Three months after they started dating, Pauline and Chris decided to make love. "It was amazing," Pauline says. "We hadn't talked much about the fact that we wanted to hold off beyond a kind of whispered, 'Hey, let's take our time.' But then one weekend in September, we planned a camping trip in the mountains, one that would obviously put us in the same tent overnight. Simply agreeing to go on the weekend amounted to agreeing to making love. And it turned out to be the most marvelous, romantic night of my life."

Pauline said she hadn't had sex with a man the entire time she'd been sober. "When I drank, I was close to completely in-discriminate. If a man had the right look or attitude, which for me meant slightly dangerous and threatening, and I was drunk enough, which I usually was, there was no question. Having sex for me was completely hooked to drinking. It was what you did when you went out on a weekend. I got into some pretty degrading scenes. Stuff that I now label as abusive. I really felt used. In sobriety, I made a vow not to hurt myself in the same way. I poured energy into my career. I developed friendships with women. In fact, for a little while, not having hooked up with a man or even met anyone I thought was attractive, I began to wonder if I might not be gay or at least bisexual. My sponsor is lesbian, and I was so moved by how close she was to her lover, moved and envious. In fact, any story of any couple riveted me. How did they meet? How did they sustain their love? How did people manage to stay together for the long haul? But for so long, I didn't feel like I had any relationship prospects. I was *very* cautious. And yet, I've come to realize, I really wanted some kind of romantic attention and contact.

"So, with Chris, I was overwhelmed. In one night, I got everything I wanted! That night, the first night we made love, was simply incredible. For Chris too; he had similarly kept himself dammed up. Well, he *had* one brief, disastrous affair with a married woman early on in his sobriety. But nothing after that. We're both in our late twenties. At the first contact in that tent, it suddenly seemed absurd to be so young and not to have been having sex every night! Which is what we ended up doing afterward. We were safe; he used a condom. But emotionally, we were completely unbridled. I've just never felt myself *fit* with anyone like Chris. Not just the actual act of intercourse, but simply falling asleep in his arms. You know how with some people it feels like cuddling up to a bunch of fence pickets? Or how this or that limb gets numb and you just feel painfully entangled? Not Chris and me. We simply *fit*. It's hard to convey the wonder of it. It's always easier to make negative stuff sound real. Trying to convey the joy of positive stuff can sound so corny or put on. But Chris and I found something incredible with each other: a physical and emotional and even spiritual sense of merging neither of us had known before. Making love sober had always filled me with apprehension. Could I let go without drinking? With Chris, there wasn't even a doubt, not a question about that. The moment our bodies touched, it was like we were home free . . . "

The experience of making love was so overwhelmingly positive for both of them that they felt they weren't only "home free" in the sexual department, but also in every other part of their lives. "We began to spend every possible free moment with each other. At first, it was wonderful. We only had to look in each other's eyes and that magic, the magic of that first night up in the mountains under the stars, was right there. But sometimes, at first almost imperceptibly, sometimes the magic wouldn't be there. And that panicked us. It's like we had decided that we had found some perfect key to happiness and we'd never have a bad moment again; we wouldn't *allow* anything to be less than perfect. What we did, I now realize, is think of each other like we used to think of alcohol: a reliable cure-all, something that would make us perfectly happy, bring

us to the same blissful state every time. Which of course alcohol never did. And which, of course, nothing ever does." The
surface of their determinedly seamless happiness began to
crack when Chris brought up the possibility of living together.
"In the abstract, that seemed okay to me," Pauline says. "But
when we actually began looking at apartments, I freaked. I
hadn't realized how much I'd come to treasure my own space,
a room of my own. As much as I loved being with Chris, I
began to realize that I also loved getting away by myself, back
to my own private little nest. I started to notice things Chris
did in his own house that I wouldn't be able to tolerate in
mine. Stuff like leaving the butter out instead of putting it
back in the refrigerator, leaving socks on the floor. We have
totally different ideas of hominess too. I like a kind of bright,
open-air, New Mexican look; he tends to clutter things up
with pictures and books and sports stuff. Suddenly, how he
kept things at home seemed to be symbolic of something more
important. He didn't seem as sensitive as he used to. He wasn't
picking up on my moods the way I'd convinced myself he always did before. He'd withdraw sometimes. Why had I never
noticed this before?

"Once I saw the first few cracks in the relationship, cracks
seemed to be all I could see. And then, I did something I'd
never done before. I've got a phone answering machine and I
almost never use it to screen calls. When I was home, every
time the phone rang, I'd always leap for it. It might be Chris!
But one Saturday morning when I expected Chris to call and
the phone rang, I let the machine pick it up. I remember just
standing there, looking down at it as it made its whirring and
clicking sounds and hearing Chris's surprised voice on the
tape, 'Pauline, honey? Where are you?' I couldn't pick the
phone up. Somehow those cracks up there at the surface had

split right down to the center of me. For the first time, I felt something terrible. *I didn't want to see Chris.*"

This was emotionally devastating to Pauline. "We had had such a perfect relationship! What had gone wrong? My sadness turned to anger and frustration. I began to attack both of us with a vengeance. First, him: he wasn't what he appeared to be. He was conventional and dull and would never be anything more exciting than an insurance salesman. What kind of romantic partner was that? Now that the pleasurable shock of having sex had worn off a bit, was there really anything left? Had we just imagined, made up the emotional closeness we said we felt? Next, I attacked me. The real problem was, I'm incapable of intimacy. If a man isn't a perfect Prince Charming, I can't tolerate it. I'm a total control freak, immature. There's no room in my life for anyone who disagrees with me in the least detail. What sort of fool am I that I think I could have a normal relationship with anyone?"

Pauline thought of her sponsor Jennifer. "I'd always thought of Jennifer as one of the few sober people I knew who was in a perfect relationship. She seemed to adore her lover Karen. As far as I knew, they never fought; they never even disagreed! They had one of the most serene relationships I'd ever seen. Suddenly, I desperately needed to talk to Jennifer, to find out how she did it, what I was doing wrong. So not five minutes after Chris called, I phoned Jennifer."

Pauline did not, however, get what she expected from the phone call. Jennifer wasn't home, and Karen answered the phone with what Pauline called an uncharacteristic "angry grunt. She sounded so upset and impatient! I wondered if the world had gone completely crazy. Karen had always been the least flappable of people. Meditative, serene, smiling benignly at whatever happened to her. But this wasn't the same lady. In the space of forty-five seconds, she told me that she didn't know where Jennifer was, probably playing handball at the gym instead of staying here to help her with the garden like she'd promised to do, she'd just about had it with Jennifer's selfishness and tantrums, and though she'd leave a note that I called, I shouldn't expect a call back anytime soon since God only knew when Jennifer would be back, Jennifer never paid attention to anything Karen told her, she'd never *known* anyone so irresponsible . . . It was like a small hurricane had gotten into the phone! I couldn't contain my shock. I just barely managed to thank Karen for passing on the message, then I hung up." This was the last straw, Pauline thought. "If the most perfect relationship I knew was falling apart, what hope could there be for anyone else, especially Chris and me?"

Pauline spent a miserable afternoon in her apartment, forcing herself to clean it, scrubbing the bathroom and kitchen floors as if the work of scrubbing would somehow clarify her own confused feelings. At about four o'clock, Jennifer did call Pauline back. Pauline cut to the chase. "What's going on between you and Karen? She nearly bit my head off his morning! Are you two having problems?" Jennifer let out an exasperated breath, part sigh, part laugh. "What we're having, dear friend, is a *relationship*. Good Lord, how I can sometimes hate that word . . . " Pauline was silent for a moment, silent and depressed. "So all relationships are impossible, huh?" she asked mournfully. "That's what I called you to have you tell me wasn't true."

Jennifer laughed, with no trace of her previous sigh. "Poor baby. Having a hard time with Mr. Right?"

Pauline said yes, she was.

"So you're finally joining the rest of us mortals? I was wondering when that might happen . . . "

Jennifer then gave what Pauline said was the first version of a "speech that I have since asked her to repeat to me every time I forget that Chris and I are human beings. Basically what she said was, all people are pains in the neck. It is hard to have a relationship with *anyone*. A lot of recovering alcoholics and addicts think they can bypass this difficulty. We decide we've had *enough* difficulty, thank you very much. Now that we're recovering, we expect some very definite rewards. Now that we're all being, or trying to be, the best little boys and girls in the world, shouldn't we be handed a few prizes? Like a wonderful job, more money, perfect health, and most of all, the soul mate we deserve? What use is there in getting sober if we're not able to live satisfying lives? Jennifer wasn't saying we didn't have the right to pursue satisfaction. In fact, Jennifer calls herself an out-and-out hedonist. 'I love food and sex and Carole Lombard movies, not necessarily in that order,' she says. 'Can't get enough of any of the three. Pleasure is wonderful. We should have scads of it! Only, we've got to see it a little differently than we used to.' Basically what Jennifer is saying is that we need to change our attitudes about getting 'rewarded.' People don't often respond the way we want them to, even if we're being the 'best' we know how to be or acting in a way that we feel deserves a certain response. The problem is that we're using alcohol as the model for the rewards we think we ought to be getting. When we drank, alcohol was a completely known given: we could always depend on it getting us high and drunk and sometimes comatose. There were no mysteries about it. It was a 'reward' we could pretty much completely depend on to have a certain predictable effect. But we learn in sobriety that other rewards aren't nearly as predictable. Sober life teaches us that we have to be flexible, that things aren't perfect, that there are any number of surprises that can happen to us, not all of them pleasant but not all of them unpleasant, either."

Pauline says, "On some level this sounds pretty obvious. I mean, I'd already realized in the years I've been sober that life isn't the black-and-white proposition that it seemed to be when I drank and smoked pot. But I'd never connected this idea of flexibility to sex and love. Jennifer said there was a simple reason for this. I hadn't had any experience with sex and love in sobriety! I hadn't given myself the same permission to make mistakes, to have things be unpredictable, that I'd given myself in my first days, weeks, months, and years of keeping away from booze and drugs. I'd paid my dues, that's what I felt. Now that I'd met a romantic partner, things were supposed to go on automatic again, return to black and white! But human beings, even human beings in love, don't play according to that script. That is what I was finding out, painfully, with Chris."

Pauline quotes something Jennifer said to her during the Saturday afternoon phone conversation: "'People are a pain in the neck, no doubt about it. But that doesn't mean you can't love them. Karen and I were at each other's throats today! But there's not a person in the world I love more than Karen. And I know, as much as she'd like to throw the nearest pot of begonias at me, Karen loves me the same way. What you learn is, just as sobriety can survive any feeling you bring to it, from joy to despair, so can love.'"

Pauline eventually called Chris back and drummed up the courage to talk to him about all this. Chris was relieved; he'd also been having some secret doubts and fears about their relationship that he wanted to talk about. "It was such a relief," Pauline says. "We'd been trying so hard to be perfect partners to each other that we didn't realize we were strangling the life out of our relationship. But now we've broken some new ice. We're more able to trust that we can survive each other's feelings, doubts, and imperfections. A very nice dividend is that our sexual relationship has, if anything, gotten freer and more satisfying. Maybe not as blazing as it was that first night in the mountains, but more comfortable, less driven and urgent. Chris actually seems like a man I might be able to *live* with, not just imagine as a kind of perfect fantasy figure. Now that we've decided to get married, I feel a kind of open-eyed acceptance I didn't feel before. I accept that our feelings won't always be positive and that that's okay, even perfectly normal. We're just more *human* than we used to let ourselves think."

CHIAROSCURO

It's one thing to accept in the abstract that "our feelings won't always be positive," but Pauline and Chris are the first to admit that they are still continually rocked by their emotions. Sometimes it's very hard to have the sense that love, like sobriety, can become a *context* for emotions, containing them rather than being destroyed by them. Understanding this at a gut level takes a kind of constant vigilance, an actively maintained consciousness that people in recovery seem to need to rev up daily.

"The fact is, a relationship is hard work," says Lennie, a truck dispatcher in Brooklyn who's been sober in AA for eight years. "So hard that for a long time, I just gave up on the whole idea after my last marriage. Granted, I was a raging drunk when I got divorced from my last wife, so I didn't know a whole hell of a lot about relationships. But I got sober soon after, and I've gone out with some women since then, and in some ways sometimes I wish I still drank. At least you could escape the whole mess when you drank. Get yourself into a stupor where nothing mattered and life turned into a game of how long it would take to pass out. But now, well, there's Allie. And she taught me this new word, painter that she is. She told me what she and I have is chiaroscuro. I told her to watch her language, first time she came out with that. She said that's just what she was doing. Then she told me what it meant.

"She says chiaroscuro means you've got both light and dark, shading, it looks three-dimensional, not just a flat picture like a kid would draw. You make a picture look *real* with this chiaroscuro. But the main thing to remember is, she tells me, it's got both dark and light. You feel like you can put your hands around it, when a picture has chiaroscuro. It's got sides and a back you can't see, like the dark side of the moon."

Accepting the dark and light of reality isn't something Lennie has liked doing very much. "Let's just get to it. Sex, I mean. I'm fifty-two years old. I look like about fifty-eight, probably. Booze kicked my ass. Every time I think of any woman looking twice at me, I gotta think she's crazy. I mean, I'm clean and all, but I'm damaged goods. The broken blood vessels in my nose aren't likely to go away any time soon. I'm not exactly in terrific shape. Got a gut. I stopped drinking because I just got too tired to put up with the messes it kept getting me into. That thing you hear in AA about getting sick and tired of being sick and tired? That's my story. But I wasn't only giving up drinking. I figured I was giving up most of the rest of life too. Like women. Until recently I've always thought it was *unnatural* or something to have sex past the age of about forty-five. People who start to sag and look old should just lay off." Lennie knows this is not a popular opinion. "When I tell my sponsor I think this, he looks at me like I'm crazy. He's married. He and his wife are in their sixties, and they go on a lot of romantic trips to Bermuda. He finally suggested to me that maybe my disgust with the idea of sex for anyone over forty-five has to do with my disgust for me. That made sense, I guess, but it didn't change much. I was just shut down in that area for good, I thought, until Allie."

Allie, Lennie says, runs a small commercial art agency that did some posters for the trucking business where Lennie works. "I wasn't supposed to have anything to do with her," Lennie says. "My boss calls me into the office one day. Allie's standing next to him by his desk, and they're both looking at these giant red-and-blue posters of trucks with smiling grilles. Ever since I got sober, my boss has really depended on me. He doesn't trust his own opinion about much of anything. The secret is, I pretty much run the place. He's always asking my advice, like I'm the only guy there who knows trucks. Well, maybe he's right. Anyway, he asks me what I think of the posters. I tell him they look lousy, like some kind of kid cartoon. He shrugs. He tells Allie that he values my opinion. Allie laughs, which makes me look at her. 'Pretty definite about it, huh?' she says. I say I tend to be pretty definite about most things. My boss tells me to go have lunch with this Allie, tell her what I think of some other ad ideas she has. And that's how we started."

Allie is forty-eight, past Lennie's cut-off point, but he had to admit that from the start, he was intrigued by her. "She's not a recovering alcoholic or a recovering anything, which means she seems like a whole different animal from me. But she has this funny kind of sense of humor. Not like she's goofing on me or anything, just that she doesn't take everything so goddamned seriously. She's pretty too. I had to admit that. She has nice thick brown hair, and she's kind of plump but in the right places. First time I met her, I began to question that thing about being too old. Well, I knew I was too old, but I could imagine a guy going for Allie, very easily."

Allie said she was impressed by Lennie's strong opinions about her ad campaign, and she asked him to look at a few other mock-ups she'd brought. "I liked one more than the others, and I told her why. It was simple and direct and looked the most professional of the three she showed me. Kind of no-nonsense, like you could rely on the company. Didn't get cute, like the others. She said she saw my point. She also said maybe I could come by and look at some other campaigns she was doing for other businesses. She'd value my opinion, she said. I made some joke about how my rates were high, was she sure she could afford me? She said she could buy me dinner. So I said yes." Lennie began going out with Allie and feeling ambivalent about it. "Allie is more than just a businesswoman, she's a real artist. She paints on her time off from work, and after the first few dates we had, she asked me up to her place to look at her stuff. Now, I don't know from art, but I really like what she paints. She does mothers and children, a lot of them, all big and fat and affectionate, like they really love each other. Some of them are naked, but it's not embarrassing. In fact, the naked women and children she paints look so at ease that they almost seem like they're wearing clothes. I liked Allie; she was different from any other woman I'd met, any other person, really. Nobody ever talked to me about art or cared what I thought about stuff like that. But I also felt wary. I was attracted to her, but every time I imagined even kissing her, I couldn't imagine her being anything but revolted by me. Who would want to kiss this mug? So we just kept it to dinners and movies and going back sometimes to her place to look at whatever painting she was working on. I think I was scared of anything else happening. I wanted to keep some distance;

that's what it boiled down to. And yet, sitting with her in her nice living room—she lives in Brooklyn Heights and it's one of these nice old-fashioned places with a fireplace and all the original moldings, looks like a museum, all pretty and deco-rated—with her there, looking at her in the light of the fire, sometimes I'd just want to reach out to her, just hold her hand. It was dark enough that she wouldn't have to worry about see-ing me too clearly. It wouldn't be so bad to hold her hand, would it? I went through a lot of that. Like a kid. Jesus, I sound like a kid . . . "

Allie finally took some initiative after a few months of dates in which Lennie couldn't bring himself even to sit close to her. "What she said was, 'Why don't you ever kiss me?' Just like that. I was really embarrassed. I said, '*I'm* supposed to be the blunt one, not you.' But she just looked at me, waiting for an answer. I couldn't believe she really wanted me to. So I asked her if she did. And she said yes. And I moved closer to her on the couch, and closed my eyes as my face got near hers, I guess because I didn't want to see what I was still sure would be the look of disappointment in her eyes, and I kissed her. She kissed me back. And she held me. And it, well, do I look like the kind of guy who cries? I didn't cry then either. But to tell you the truth, I felt like it. Because nobody had ever touched me like that since—since when? It felt like never. When I had sex with my two ex-wives, and before that in the army with this or that woman I picked up, I was drunk. I never knew, not once in my life, what it was like to kiss someone sober!"

Lennie says it shook him. "It was like the tables turned. Here I am, the big old experienced guy; I'm supposed to be calling the shots, right? But I was like a little kid, like a virgin or something! She sort of took over, and I let her. I tried not to think of what I looked like to her. I could tell from her kiss that she wasn't nauseated, so maybe it was okay. But she was so beautiful to me, and so gentle; it's like she could tell how much I was hurting inside. I didn't even know I was hurting that much inside until she touched me. I guess that's why I felt like crying a little. But, hey, we were a grown man and woman, even if we were beyond my cut-off age of forty-five, and she was so beautiful, and this old urge, this feeling for a woman that I'd buried so deep in me, it finally started to come up again. And I took the reins back. I don't know where I got the courage, but my arms went around her, and it felt like she sort of surrendered to me. We both wanted to make love, there was no doubt any more about that. And, well, we did. Right there in front of the fireplace."

Lennie says he felt humbled by the experience and by his subsequent experiences of making love with Allie. "It gets deeper and deeper every time. I don't know how to explain it. It's like God gave me something I desperately wanted before I even knew I wanted it or believed I could have it. But the pleasure of it—it's like nothing I've ever experienced. For one thing, I'm *sober*. There's nothing between me and my feelings. I'm just not used to that! Stuff comes up like I never expected. Sometimes, out of nowhere, Allie and I will laugh! It won't be like we're ticklish or anything. We'll just look at each other and find everything incredibly funny! And sometimes, you know, the lust will be so crazy that I think I'm gonna go out of my mind, and she's right there with me. It's like we're riding a race car over a smooth highway—nothing can stop us! And then we'll slow down, start to feel a little shy maybe, like kids again. And I'll feel like I've never touched her before, like I can find places on her body I never knew were there, that she never knew were there. There are all these things, always some new way to touch each other. And the kicker is— first of all that I'm talking like this! Who'd have predicted that? I'm not even supposed to be having sex, not according to *my* rules! But the bigger thing is, I'm having feelings and thoughts I never imagined I'd have, not just about sex, but about Allie and me and, not to sound too hokey, about how *life* works. This thing with Allie, it's not all happy-happy pleasure. Sometimes when I'm with her, I feel so incredibly sad. Like I said, I'm not the kind of guy who cries. But I'll tell you a secret. One time we were together, I bawled like a baby. And I don't even know why. It was just that she touched me somehow. It was more than physical; it was like we were together so completely that I didn't know where I was. I'm getting so much more than I ever dreamed. When I hear in AA that your life will be something beyond your wildest dreams— that's the literal *truth*, man! But this sadness. It's like, be very careful of what you want, because it's going to be attached to so much more than you bargained for. I feel like I'm talking like a lunatic, but I'll say these things to Allie and she'll understand. She'll say that thing about chiaroscuro. That we're giving each other all the light and dark that's in us. And that there's always more where that came from. 'Always more roundness,' she says. Ever since Allie came into my life, I feel like I'm part of the universe in a way I never was before. And it's not only that she gives *me* something. I know I'm giving her something too. I'm not an ugly troll. I'm a man, I'm sexual, I'm emotional, I've got a lot to give, and I can receive a lot too. Wonder how many other truck dispatchers can say the same thing? Well, if they're recovering drunks, they've got the same chance I had to find all this out."

Lennie says he doesn't know where his relationship with Allie is going. "She says she doesn't want to get married, which throws me a little, because as screwed up as my life has been, I have some pretty old-fashioned morals, like you're supposed to marry the woman you go to bed with." But over the past six months that they've been making love, he's begun to accept the open-endedness of their relationship; it feels like it's okay. "You know, Allie says we've got to invent our lives. Sort of figure out what makes us happy, and then follow that. It's not like she's some irresponsible free spirit who doesn't care about what she does. She's a real reliable woman in business, and she's devoted to me. But she wants to keep things open. She says we should explore pleasure, find out what's in each of us, just enjoy that, and be kind to each other. For now, we don't need to go beyond that. I tend to want to control things, know what's going to happen. I'm scared of losing her. I really worry, what if she gets bored with me, wakes up to how old and ugly I am? It's like this scared little baby woke up in me. It's so hard to just accept the pleasure we've got and not make plans to sort of pin it down. But maybe that's what this is teaching me. You can't pin this kind of thing down. You can't freeze feelings, keep them exactly the same. Every time I make love with Allie, it feels new. I'm always amazed that it's so wonderful, and in ways that feel completely new! Maybe this sounds too good to be true. But it *is* the truth. Who knows where we'll go with all this. I only know this woman has taught me more about love in six months than I learned in my previous fifty-two years. I know something else too. None of this could possibly be happening if I weren't sober."

SEX, LAUGHTER, AND MORTALITY: MEETING YOUR HIGHER POWER IN BED

Pleasure in sobriety has chiaroscuro: darks and lights, three dimensions. Every recovering man and woman I've talked to who has found satisfaction in lovemaking affirms this. "It's like the sun is *finally* shining," says one woman I know who, after a tumultuous ten years of marriage, only the past four of which she's been sober, has managed in the past few months to reconnect with her husband sexually. "But it's not high noon. It's not some blasting brightness that erases everything. It's the sun right after dawn or late in the afternoon: plenty of light, but plenty of shadow as well. Things stand out in this light; they don't disappear in it. It's pleasure that somehow has *room* for my feelings. Sure, sometimes I mourn the old blast, which is what alcohol and drugs gave me at the best times. Everything was flattened when I got high. The idea was to get to this simple, zonked-out state of bliss where no negative feeling was even possible. That's not what pleasure is like for me now. Pleasure is happening in *reality*. But amazingly, that doesn't mean it's a letdown." Like Lennie, this woman has discovered a far richer capacity for experiencing pleasure than she ever could, drunk or high. It's a pleasure that can contain and draw on her feelings, not a pleasure that depends on blocking them out.

As we've seen in all the stories in this book, increasing our capacity for this kind of pleasure takes time and patience and an abundance of compassion for what are usually the lifelong blocks and fears we struggle against. We learn that our capacity to enjoy sexual pleasure is inextricably connected to our capacity to let up on, accept, and love ourselves. Lennie's experience is telling because it reveals that this flowering of capacity has its own timetable: it happens at a moment of readiness, a moment he could never have willed or planned, a moment to which he was led first by staying sober, second by allowing himself to risk opening himself up to a kiss. It's exasperating, sometimes, to accept this, as we realize how powerless we are to speed up or slow down our timetables: we can't will ourselves to "flower" on cue. Recovering people teach me that all we can do is cultivate the soil of our sobriety, plant what seeds we can find, and pretty much let go of what sprouts up and how long it takes to come to fruition.

This is something Bill and his lover Don, both recovering alcoholics, have learned over the fifteen years they've been together. Bill is, by his own reckoning, in the "active dying stage" of his battle with AIDS. "I don't know how you spend your Saturday afternoons," Bill says, "but if you want to find me, I'll be in the corridor of the fourth floor of Building D at the county hospital hooked up to an IV, getting my new dose of blood for the week, fighting the good fight against anemia. Need those red blood cells, man. Like a fix. There's some kind of metaphor in there: going from my fix of bourbon to my fix of blood. It's like I need something more vital than alcohol to keep me alive. I need something a lot more nurturing than getting wasted."

Bill and Don are in their mid forties, and Bill has been sober for the past nine years. "I was diagnosed with the HIV virus about five years ago," he says. "I probably had it for a lot longer than that. I went in because I was coughing and losing weight, and it turned out I was well on the way to developing PCP, the pneumonia associated with AIDS. I was in a lot of denial before that. I'd stopped drinking, I was going to the gym, I was being monogamous with Don. Well, there were two or three brief encounters in the sauna of my gym, but they were safe. They were just playing around, nothing serious. I was taking care of myself. And I just decided, somehow, that because I'd turned a new leaf, God wouldn't play any tricks on me. Getting sober is all about giving yourself a second chance, right? I couldn't possibly have AIDS. It just wouldn't be fair."

The past five years have been, in Bill's words, "a roller coaster. I almost lost it at first, almost started drinking again.

God *had* played a trick. He had a hell of a sense of humor. I was in a rage about my health, a rage that was fueled by terrible fear. I had so many plans! Ever since I'd stopped drinking, I had this whole new sense of vision in my life. I was saving money to be able to quit my job at a travel agency so I could set myself up in my own business as a private travel consultant. Don and I were looking at houses with the idea of buying; all we'd ever lived in were rented places. I had these wonderful fantasies of getting old: traveling when I wanted to, having a sort of happy long marriage with Don. Stuff had improved so much between us after I got sober, Don was so supportive; I couldn't have been more grateful. And here I was with AIDS. And in a pretty advanced stage of it."

Bill said that in the first year, one of the first casualties in his life with Don was their sex life. "All the old guilt, the old self-hate, the old internalized homophobia I'd felt throughout my life but thought I'd gotten over came back; I hadn't gotten over it. It seemed that all sex could do was kill you. I cringed every time Don touched me. I just went spiralling down into this awful bitterness and self-hate. The hate extended to AA and going to meetings and all of what now sounded like crap in the Twelve Steps. When I said anything in a meeting, which wasn't often, it was bitter and snide. I took everybody's inventory. How dare they complain about their curtains and their cats? I know now that this was a stage I needed to go through, this self-hate, self-pity. But I couldn't have anticipated what would break it. I've lost a lot of friends to AIDS. I used to wonder if it weren't some kind of dementia associated with the disease that changed the personality of so many of them. One of the earmarks of the disease, at least for a lot of the guys I knew, was that all your bitterness was released. Here you wanted to comfort a guy, make him feel better, say nice things to him, accentuate the positive, and he wasn't having any of it. A lot of guys who used to be sweet and tolerant and funny turned into petty tyrants, complaining about everything: food, friends, the weather, and above all their treatment at the hands of doctors, clinics, and hospitals. I didn't want to turn into that kind of bitter person, but that's exactly what I was doing."

Bill says that a turning point happened because of two things. "I was ready to give up my self-pity, and Don was ready to help me replace it with something else." The "something else" had to do with sex. "Our sex life had never been a raging turn-on for me," Bill says. "What happened to us is what I know happens to a lot of couples who've been with each other for a long time. Sex was a kind of friendly, comfortable thing, something that gave you a kind of predictable release, something like sinking into the same old easy chair. I'd spice things up even in sobriety sometimes by putting on a porno tape or going out on my own to this or that late night club when Don was out of town, which he sometimes had to be for business reasons. But when I got sick, that comfortable chair just disgusted me. It wasn't that I didn't sometimes want sex. God, sometimes I'd have these incredible erotic dreams, really outrageous stuff: tackling some lifeguard on the beach and rolling around naked in the breaking waves, making love to my high school geometry teacher in the middle of sophomore midterms, locking the door to my doctor's office and stripping my doctor's clothes off him. And I'd wake up, raging for an orgasm. Sometimes I'd masturbate, but sometimes I wouldn't. It was like I felt filled with some evil, malignant fluid. Do you have any idea what it feels like to think your insides are *toxic*? In some emotional way, it was as if what I'd always secretly feared about myself was now proven to be true: I was rotten and evil inside, and if you got anywhere near my bodily fluids, it would kill you. That's how bad I was! My disease was some kind of embodiment of self-hate. So when I had a sexual urge, it just seemed like some kind of evil trick my body was playing on me, something to get me to infect somebody else! That was the truth: sex equaled infection, at least when it had anything to do with me."

Bill had a breakthrough in what he called "the least likely place: a crowded triple room in the hospital I'd been moved into after Don took me to the emergency room when the pneumonia seemed to be coming back and I was having a hard time breathing." Bill says he was really scared. "This was the third time the pneumonia came back, and I'd known a lot of guys who didn't survive the third time. I was a wreck. Don was great. He just bundled me up, actually bodily picked me up, and shoved me into a cab, took over completely, got through the red tape, and had me seen to immediately, which in the emergency room of this county hospital on a Friday night was no mean feat."

Bill was hooked up to "several IVs, shoved under a mask with aerosol Pentamadine for the pneumonia—in other words, back into the Rube Goldberg contraption of a hospital bed with its tubes and screens and monitors and beeps and smells and voices and groans from neighboring beds. It was all beginning to seem like home to me, I'd been through this stuff so many times. But I was scared. I really didn't think I'd come out of this. I kept thinking: 'this is it.'

"Don stayed with me until I dropped off to sleep, which somehow I finally did. Then, late at night, it must have been past midnight—I don't know how Don managed to convince the floor nurse to let him stay past visiting hours but he managed it—I woke up. The hospital was pretty quiet. Don was sitting real close to me as I opened my eyes. He'd pulled the curtain shut around my bed. There were two other beds in the room, fully occupied with snoring sick bodies. I opened my eyes and saw Don's big goofy face grinning first at me, then at the tent-pole thing sticking up in the middle of my bed. Evidently I was having one of my raging erotic dreams again. He said, 'Well, one part of you is doing just fine.' Now here I am, not exactly at my sexiest, with tubes coming out of various veins, a mask over my face, sprawled out in the faint green light of a hospital room, but for some reason, and I swear I don't know why, I had the most incredible urge to have some kind of sex right then with Don. There wasn't a lot we could do, given the setup we were in. But I asked him anyway, 'So what are you gonna do about it?' Deftly, silently, he removed my sheet and revealed the one happy part of me. And let's just say that he gave me an awfully long, warm, and delightful, er, *hand*shake." Bill laughs at the memory. "God, this was *not* a porno movie. I mean, this is not what most people, even if they're into bondage, get turned on by! I kept wondering what the sixty-year-old blue-haired nurse who was out at the reception desk would do if she knew what was going on. I didn't have to wait long to find out. As the happy part of me rose to unbearable happiness, I groaned loudly enough to lure her in. The curtains were flung back. Don's hand had shot back, but he hadn't had time to replace the sheet. Talk about mommy coming in and finding out what you're really doing instead of homework. 'What on earth is going on here?' she asked, inanely. It had to be pretty obvious. Don didn't miss a beat. 'We're exercising.' She was such a mass of flutters and embarrassment; she sort of snorted like a horse and announced that visiting hours could no longer be extended. But then even she seemed to see something funny in it. She paused and there was a flicker of a smile in her face. 'Gym class is *over*,' she finally said."

Bill recovered from this last bout of pneumonia, and is back home now, feeling he's recovered in another way as well. "Look, I know I don't probably have a lot of time left. But I've still got spirit left. God only knows why I was able to break through my self-pity and self-hate when I was. All I know is, things are different now. My life has humor back in it. Somehow, even in the face of what I guess is supposed to be a tragedy—me having AIDS—things don't seem so all-fired *serious* any more. I feel like Don and I are learning to take advantage of all kinds of moments. I have this image sometimes of us being two little kids, blowing bubbles, trying to catch each one, looking at each incredibly beautiful iridescent orb before it bursts, enjoying them, laughing at them when they look, for an instant, like an elephant or a pancake, delighting that there are more bubbles after that. Things seem so sort of translucent now. I'm appreciating the beauty of life as I accept its fragility. And sexually, well, I'm simply *back* now. The self-hate, the fear have lifted. Sure, I've got my rhythms. Waking up and wanting to have sex confirms a pattern with me: I'm usually aroused when I just wake up. And Don is learning to take advantage of these times. We're seeing the fun in things. There's a kind of gentle humor here that's turning out to be the most healing thing I know. They say in AA that all recovery is spiritual. Now I know on a gut level exactly what that means. When I wake up in the morning and for the moment feel good, my emotions and spirit sort of rush in to rejoice. What incredible joy it is to experience this beauty again."

Appreciating just how dark, buried, and confusing our sexual fears and resistances can be has made my work in this book very humbling. It's clear to me that there is no way I can have done justice to the full power and complication of sex in recovering people's lives. My goal here has been to offer something basic: a call to consciousness, to the awakening, that it's all right, in fact *necessary* to our well-being and sobriety, to begin the process of sexual self-exploration, acceptance, and honesty, whatever mesh of sexual circumstances and feelings we may each privately be dealing with. More simply: *it's all right to be who you are right now.* A wonderful dividend of cultivating this self-acceptance is that it allows our sexual selves to seek their own appropriate and satisfying means of expression. We don't have to do much about it! When we let out who we are, those newly freed selves begin to decide for *themselves* how they want to live. There's no need to plan or worry or coerce. How we want to be sexually, or in any other aspect of our lives, will come organically out of a full, free acceptance of who we are. Every man and woman in this book bears witness to this.

But maybe, even after all you've read in this book, this all sounds like easy platitudes. We're used to giving lip service to the idea that we need to be honest and self-accepting. But most of us are frightened out of our wits by the prospect of being completely honest, especially about sex, at a *gut* level. What I hope most is that in this book I've given you evidence that this honesty isn't as toxic as you might once have feared. Every person you've met in this book was desperately afraid of facing and revealing who he or she was inside. By their example, you can see that, with patience and compassion, this fear can be assuaged.

Once the fear is assuaged, even to the smallest degree, a new kind of light will guide us. Everyone in this book has spoken of this. To paraphrase the woman I quoted earlier in this chapter: in sobriety, the sun begins to shine, but not so blindingly that you can't see. Pleasure, like the rest of life in sobriety, has *roundness*: lights and darks, contrasts—chiaroscuro.

There is an enormous range of feeling—fear and joy, boredom and apprehension—an enormous palette of emotional color we bring to every experience as we get sober. As we face our sexual fantasies, our perceptions of our physical bodies, our romantic obsessions, our fears and demons and blocks, we discover that there are no right or wrong ways to experience pleasure. Perhaps the happiest discovery of all is that pleasure is not something to feel guilty about. In fact, many of us are coming to feel that pleasure is something God (or whatever you may call your Higher Power) *wants us to have as much of as we can get.*

The Twelve Steps offer us a great deal of help in learning to meet ourselves in these deeper and richer ways and accept that satisfaction, happiness, and pleasure are all things we are meant to have. The idea of taking our own inventory, turning it over, and putting the emphasis on what we can give to, rather than squeeze out of, the world gives us profoundly healing guidance as our lives become more open in sobriety. *Open* is the operative word. We become open not through the grim exercise of duty, obligation, or self-coercion, but through a sense of surrender, release, and joy. The ability to make love consciously is the product of rejoicing, as fully as we can, in our own sobriety: the consciousness that makes our lives possible. In that spirit of rejoicing, sex and love are not something to fear. They are something to cherish.

ACKNOWLEDGMENTS

More gratitude than I know how to express goes to the many recovering alcoholics and addicts I've met and listened to across the country and in England, men and women who teach me by their example and their words that satisfying sex and love are not only possible for us, but they are also some of the greatest and most revelatory adventures we can have in sober life.

It is a particular thrill for me to have occasioned with this book an unprecedented marriage between my copublishers, HarperSanFrancisco and Hazelden. Thanks go to the extraordinary and supportive crew at HarperSanFrancisco, particularly my editor Barbara Moulton, whom I treasure for her heart, humor, and abundant good sense, and her assistant Lisa Bach; and a large dose of gratitude for the all too unsung labors of production editor Rosana Francescato, whose copyediting cleaned up the syntax not only in this book but in all three of my previous Harper sobriety books. Thanks go as well as to my friend, editor Bill Chickering at Hazelden, who has given me so much support. Connie Clausen, agent and friend, who has believed in me and promoted my career with unflagging enthusiasm for a decade (sometimes against considerable odds), has my love and gratitude too.

Reuven Closter, C.S.W., the best therapist in the world, my psychological "sieve" and friend: I thank him for the insights he's helped me reach, insights that have helped me hear the people whose stories fill this book.

Sobriety has given me the gift of meeting, loving, and working with so many people, men and women, friends, family, colleagues, and lovers. Joseph, Donna, Peter, Laura, Catherine, Ingrid, Quentin, Frank, Chris, Orese, Allen, Ross, Hubertus, Lew, my parents Carl and Alice, and Richard—I owe each such a special and unique debt. They have done nothing less than teach me how to love. How can I tally up my gratitude to them? All I know how to do right now is say that I love them, with all my heart.

And thanks to my brother, to whom this book is dedicated and who, in spirit, keeps reminding me that life is about joy.